Why ~~...~~ Necessary

Frankly, adults have had their own way for too long. If kids want to do anything they have to get permission from an adult. Why? Because adults are in charge. But why are they in charge? Because they are more intelligent? No, most adults haven't got the brain of a grass-hopper. The reason is that adults are

(a) bigger
(b) have all the money

The trouble is, they own where we live and dictate what we wear, what we eat and where we go. And because they are bigger and have all the money, they think they can pick our friends, decide how we look, what time we go to bed, and even how we breathe ('Don't breathe through your mouth, it's bad for you').

This book tells you how to beat them, so use it and learn to rule your world. Don't let them get you down!

KIDS RULE OK!

The
Complete
HOW TO HANDLE
GROWN-UPS

Jim and Duncan Eldridge

Illustrated by
David Mostyn

RED FOX

A Red Fox Book
Published by Random Century Children's Books
20 Vauxhall Bridge Road, London SW1V 2SA

A division of the Random Century Group
London Melbourne Sydney Auckland
Johannesburg and agencies throughout the world

Red Fox edition 1991

How to Handle Grown-Ups
First published by Beaver Books 1985
Text © Jim and Duncan Eldridge 1985
Illustrations © The Hutchinson Publishing Group 1985

What Grown-Ups Say and What They Really Mean
First published by Beaver Books 1986
Text © Jim and Duncan Eldridge 1986
Illustrations © David Mostyn 1986

More Ways To Handle Grown-Ups
First published by Beaver Books 1987
Text © Jim and Duncan Eldridge 1987
Illustrations © Century Hutchinson Limited 1987

Printed and bound in Great Britain by
Cox & Wyman Ltd, Reading

ISBN 0 09 991780 7

1. HOW TO HANDLE GROWN-UPS

Reasons for not having done the washing up/washed.

There was a spider in the sink and I didn't want to kill it.

I was just about to when the Water Board phoned to say they were turning the water off, and not to use it again until further notice.

My conscience wouldn't allow me to while half the world is suffering from drought.

When I touched the tap I got an electric shock, so I thought it safest to wait.

The water came out a funny colour.

My teacher told me today that soap is made from whales, and as I've decided to become a vegetarian I can't use it.

My skin's allergic to the fluoride in the water.

I don't think it's hygienic to use our water because it's been recycled. My teacher said five people have already drunk our water before it reaches us.

I was afraid to wash up in case I broke something.

Due to the water shortage I thought it was more patriotic to save it.

First the washing-up water was too hot, so I let it cool down. Then it was too cold to get things clean.

We've run out of washing-up liquid.

I've cut my hand and the soap/washing-up liquid might get in the cut.

REasons for being late for school.

The bus had a puncture and we had to push it into the garage.

Signals from space satellites have been interfering with my digital alarm clock, so it went off an hour late.

I stopped to help an old lady across the road, then I couldn't get back because of the heavy traffic.

I was here much earlier, but no one else was, so I went home again thinking school must have been cancelled.

I got on the wrong bus.

I was doing my biology project and I wanted to see if I could wake up automatically at 7.30. I couldn't.

There was room for only one more on the bus, so although I was first in the queue I let this old lady have my place.

I was just about to leave the house when my pet cat/dog/tortoise/budgerigar fainted, and I had to revive it.

I thought my dentist/doctor's appointment was this morning, but when I got there I found it wasn't.

The kitchen cupboard collapsed on my Gran, and I had to get it off her before I came to school. I might get a 'Blue Peter' Award for saving her life.

The bus driver collapsed at the wheel and we had to wait for another bus.

The bus was hijacked.

They said on the news that all schools were closed because the teachers/caretakers/lollipop ladies were on strike.

On my paper round, I spotted a burning building and I phoned the Fire Brigade. Because I was a witness I had to wait and give evidence.

This can also be reworked as:

On my paper round, I saw a car accident and I phoned the ambulance. Because I was a witness I had to wait and give evidence.

or as:

On my paper round, I saw a break-in and I phoned the police. Because I was a witness . . . etc, etc.

I stopped on my way to deliver a message for my mother, and when I came out someone had stolen my bike.

My bike had a puncture and I had to push it to school.

The chain/handlebars/saddle came off my bike.

We were burgled in the night and I had to wait for the police to call to give my statement.

It snowed in our street this morning.

I thought today was a Bank Holiday.

I tripped on the doorstep as I was leaving and sprained my ankle.

When I left home I realized I'd left my homework indoors. I'd left my key indoors, so I had to break in, because I didn't want to come to school without my homework. I went round the house looking for a window that was open, but the only one that was open was upstairs, so I went to the shed to get my dad's ladder, but the shed was locked, so I had to break into the shed. I got the ladder out and put it against the wall and climbed up, but the ladder wasn't long enough, so I started to climb up the ivy . . . All right, I'll sit down, but don't you want to listen to my reason, sir/miss?

Excuses for having broken crockery.

The cat/dog/hamster/budgerigar did it.

It was like that when I came in.

My teacher said you could do that with it and it wouldn't break because of centrifugal force. It's my teacher's fault and I'll tell him/her he/she owes you a new cup/plate/saucer.

As I looked at it, it jumped off the shelf. I think I must have supernatural powers.

I thought it was made of unbreakable plastic.

I was trying out a science experiment I saw on 'Blue Peter'.

I don't know how it happened. I heard this crash, and there it was.

I was making you a cup of tea when it happened.

I was practising plate spinning to get into the *Guinness Book of Records*. I wanted you to be proud of me.

You said you never liked that vase/jug/cup/plate.

There must be something in the water that weakens it, because as I put it in the washing-up it just fell apart.

It was obviously faulty when it was made. In fact, I remember it had 'second' written on the bottom.

Earthenware/stoneware always breaks after six months. It's to do with the chemical nature of the soil from which it's made.

How to get more pocket money.

Everyone else gets twice as much pocket money as me. I always tell them that you can't afford to give me more because we're a very poor family.

To Mum:
I want to buy Dad a present.

To Dad:
I want to buy Mum a present.

This only works if your Mum and Dad like each other. If they don't use this variation:

I want to buy *you* a special present.

I need more pocket money so I can practise how to handle my finances for when I'm older.

My pocket money hasn't kept up with inflation. (In this case 'inflation' doesn't mean blowing up a balloon. If your suspicious parents test you by asking what inflation means, look scornful and say 'I thought you'd know already.')

I need more money because I'm saving for a set of encyclopaedias.

I need extra money because I've decided to put some money each week in to a Building Society so that when you are old I can look after you.

13

I've decided to give some money each week to charity. (Use whatever your parents' favourite charity is.)

The bus fares have gone up.

Look and Learn has gone up.

I've decided to give up sweets and things that are bad for my teeth, so I'm only going to buy things from the health food shop. Unfortunately they cost twice as much money, but if you'd prefer my teeth to decay, I'll understand.

My dentist says I've got to eat fruit. The trouble is the only fruit I like is kiwi fruit and they're very expensive.

My friends say you're mean, but I say you're not. Can I have more pocket money?

How to get your parents to buy you something.

Can you buy me this (whatever)? I'd buy it myself but I'm saving my own money to buy you a Christmas present.

My teacher says it's vital for my education.

Do you want me to be the happiest person in the world, or do you want me to look unhappy and make your life miserable?

If you buy me this bike/guitar/piano/computer, I'll be able to earn thousands with it, and then I'll be financially independent.

Everyone else has got one.

Were you a deprived child?

It would be better if you buy it for me now as an early birthday present, because if you wait till my birthday the price will go up.

Can I have these/this new shoes/trousers/ haircut. My friends say the reason I walk around looking like this is because you're mean, but I say you're just poor.

It's an investment.

Reasons For Not Eating certain foods.

My conscience won't let me eat it while half the world is starving.

A doctor on TV said that sort of food is bad for you.

I feel sick.

They use deadly pesticides to spray these vegetables.

It's too salty, and too much salt is bad for you.

It's too sweet, and too much sugar is bad for you.

I hear there was a leak in a nuclear power station near where these vegetables are grown/ animals graze.

I'm on a diet.

I've become a vegetarian/vegan/Buddhist/ Muslim/Jew/Hindu.

Our school welfare officer says too much food is bad for you.

Your cooking is really scrummy but I'd feel guilty if I gluttonized myself on it.

I've got a loose filling so I've got to avoid hard food.

A boy in our class who ate this is in hospital with food poisoning.

I'm allergic to carrots/cabbage/semolina, etc.

I saw something move in the salad.

This meat pie was once a sweet little lamb/cute baby piglet/happy fluffy chicken.

I don't eat fish – think of all the nuclear and chemical waste and oil spillages in the sea.

I had a pet rabbit/duck once. It was my best friend.

Potatoes/meat/everything gives you heart disease.

Eggs are baby chickens. I'd feel like a cannibal.

How to get MORE FOOD.

You don't want me to suffer from *anorexia nervosa,* do you?

I'm a growing child and my body needs more nourishment.

With so many people dying of starvation in the world, it would be a crime to waste food, so I've got to eat as much as I can.

Food gives you body fat, and with our cold winters I need more if I'm to keep healthy.

Your cooking is the best in the universe, it cries out to be eaten.

You're looking a little overweight, so perhaps I'd better eat that for you.

Someone else ate my first helping while I wasn't looking.

It'll go bad if we don't eat it all now.

It loses its flavour if it's left more than a day.

The chart in this health magazine said I should be much heavier for my height.

I couldn't taste that first lot of pie because I put too much salt on it.

I should eat 2000 calories a day, and I'm 400 short.

The more food I eat the more energy I'll have to help around the house.

At my friend's house they have bigger helpings than this.

The NSPCC came to school today to check if anyone was suffering from malnutrition.

Reasons for not handing in homework.

I left it on the table and the dog/cat/hamster chewed it up.

I didn't realize you'd given us any.

I did do it but Mum accidentally put it on the fire thinking it was waste paper.

We were burgled in the night and it was stolen.

My Dad thought my essay was so good he sent it to the *Guardian*. As soon as they return it I'll bring it in.

The cat was sick on it. I cleaned it up but it smelt so much my Mum wouldn't let me bring it in.

I handed it in and left it on your desk. Have you lost it?

I left it on the bus.

I thought we didn't have to hand it in until tomorrow.

My pen ran out.

I hurt my hand last night going home from school.

My brother filled my pen with vanishing ink for a joke, and when I got up this morning all my writing had vanished.

We had a power cut last night.

Reasons for WATCHING TV.

If everyone stopped watching TV, all the people who make the programmes would be out of work. I don't like watching TV all the time, but you wouldn't want me to be responsible for people losing their jobs, would you?

It's educational.

It's exercise for my eyes.

I'm watching this film because there's an educational nature programme on after it (in an hour and a half).

My friend's cousin's brother knows the man who writes this programme, and he asked me to tell him what I thought of it.

It's only got another five minutes to go before it ends.

I thought the picture went funny, so I'm watching it to see if it happens again.

They're advertising a £5000 prize if you can answer just one question, so I'm waiting for it to come on.

There's an actor/actress in this programme who looks just like you.

Dad/Mum said we're going to have to get rid of the telly, so I'm watching it while I've got the chance.

I'm doing a sponsored TV watch for charity.

This programme is the last in the series. I *can't* miss it!

REASONS FOR NOT DOING SHOPPING

I can't reach the top shelves.

The manager suspects all young people of shoplifting, so they won't let me in without an adult.

I can't read your writing on this shopping list.

Is this one potato or one pound of potatoes?

Granny always pays me for going shopping.

Last time I went you didn't give me enough money.

The shopping bag cuts my fingers.

It's half-day closing today.

The supermarket's closed for redesigning/staff training.

Does 60p taken from a pound leave 20p change?

When you say 'big tin of tomatoes' do you mean very big, large, big medium, medium or small?

I've hurt my leg/arm/ankle.

That was the shop where there was an armed robbery last week.

That shopkeeper cheats young people out of their change.

Of course I'll go shopping for you but don't blame me if I get the wrong brand.

Reason Reasons clothes are torn / soaked / damaged.

I saved someone from drowning. I might get a 'Blue Peter' Award.

I got caught in a hurricane.

I used my coat to put out a dangerous fire.

An old lady was about to be run over. I rushed forward and threw her out of the way, but I got run over myself.

I got mugged.

I got caught in the rain.

I was walking past a fire engine when its hoses burst and water went all over me.

This machine for painting white lines on roads blew up outside our school.

I was savaged by a dog/cat/werewolf.

I was standing under this drainpipe when it collapsed.

It was foggy and I fell down a hole in the road.

I was waiting at a bus stop and this car went through a puddle and splashed me.

A chemistry experiment at school went wrong.

Someone spilled ink on my jacket, and so as not to upset you I tried to clean it off myself. My friend told me acid would remove it.

What jacket?

It was either a seagull or a pigeon that did it.

How to get out of doing household chores.

I'm allergic to dust.

My elbow/leg/arm/wrist/neck hurts.

My bed *is* made.

The doctor said I've got to rest.

I've got/I'm recovering from flu.

The broom falls apart whenever I use it.

I didn't know this was your new blouse, I thought it was a duster.

How do you work the vacuum cleaner without it breaking?

The neighbours asked me if I knew the phone number of the NSPCC.

Why do we need to clean the windows? They only get dirty again.

It's not *my* dust on the floor, why should I have to sweep it up?

Does your nylon blouse go on 'boil' wash?

I don't mind doing the cooking, but last week my friend cut his/her finger off with a kitchen knife.

I did feed the goldfish. I fed it to the cat.

I've done the stew for dinner. I used that tin of meat with a picture of a cat on it.

Reasons for not having bought a Birthday card/present.

I didn't think you'd like to be reminded that you're getting older.

I don't have enough pocket money to buy you a present.

Instead of buying you a present I sent the money to your favourite charity. I thought you'd prefer that.

They didn't have a card good enough for you.

You always say it's the thought that counts.

I've sent away for your present to a mail-order company. I told them when your birthday was, but it hasn't arrived yet.

I sent it to you a week ago. I hope it hasn't got lost in the post.

I bought you a (whatever), but then I found out that Mum/Dad had bought you one as well.

As I was wrapping it up, it broke.

Mum/Dad wouldn't let me give it to you because he/she said you were allergic to it.

I didn't know your size.

I've been saving up for this special thing for you, but when I'd got all the money together the shop had sold out.

The present got stolen.

As I was writing the card my pen broke and
ruined it, so I had to throw it away.

I thought your birthday was next week.

I thought you said you didn't want me to get you
anything.

reasons for not going to skool.

I feel ill.

The teachers/caretakers/dinner ladies are on strike today.

The school's shut for the elections.

I haven't got my PE/games equipment.

As it's a public holiday today, the schools are closed.

35

There's an epidemic of measles/chicken-pox/ plague at school.

There's a bully at school who says he's going to get me.

They're decorating the school and they've found asbestos in the walls.

My teacher says I needn't come in today if I haven't done my homework.

Three children in our class have got head lice.

Our teacher's ill and they aren't getting a replacement till tomorrow.

Someone said the torrential rain last night has closed the school.

The fifth year are having exams so we don't need to go in.

Reasons for not giving up your seat on a bus.

I'm saving it for my Mum.

I've hurt my leg.

I'm actually an elderly dwarf.

There's chewing gum on this seat and I'm stuck to it.

Reasons for staying up late.

I need to stay up late so that I won't wake up early and disturb you.

I'm staying up late to see if I can get into the *Guinness Book of Records* for going without sleep for longer than anybody.

I'm getting older now so I don't need so much sleep.

I've got used to staying up late.

All my friends go to bed later than me.

There's a programme on later tonight that our teacher wants us to watch.

I thought you liked my company.

It's lonely/cold upstairs in my room.

I'll go up as soon as this programme finishes.

I've got to tidy up my room first.

The cat's just been sick on my bed.

I don't feel tired.

My head hurts when I lie down.

There's a spider/moth/ghost in my room.

I can't sleep because of the noise from the neighbours next door.

I think there are bedbugs/fleas from the cat/dog/hedgehog in my mattress.

I'm waiting for my electric blanket to heat up.

Will you read me a story?

You and I never get a chance to talk.

39

It's bad to sleep on a full stomach, and I've just eaten a sandwich.

I can't sleep when I'm hungry.

I had an electric shock last night when I turned my light on.

REASONS FOR HAVING a PET.

A dog will guard the house against burglars.

A cat will keep mice away.

A pet will teach me to be kind to animals.

They're killing stray cats/dogs at the animal home.

A canary will tell us if there's a gas leak.

All my friends have got pets.

I want an Alsation so that I can win Cruft's Dog Show, become rich and famous and then help you financially.

If you have an animal you get on 'Blue Peter'.

A tortoise is no trouble and doesn't have to be taken for long walks.

I promise I'll look after it.

If we have a dog, next door's cat will stop coming into our garden.

And if you still don't like the fish/rabbit, we can always eat it.

If I had a parrot I could teach it to talk and hire it out for films.

Taking a dog for walks would be good exercise for me.

A dog would fetch your papers for you.

A pet would be a friend for me.

A cockerel will wake me up in the morning and make sure I get up for school.

Reasons for Breaking/ Damaging/ Tearing Household Objects.

I know who did it but I'd rather not say because I don't want to get Dad/Mum in trouble.

I thought you said you were going to throw it away, anyway.

It was working when I finished with it.

The Salvation Army came round collecting jumble so I gave it to them because I thought you didn't want it any more.

I thought it was the *old* one.

You said you wanted me to be a record breaker.

The cat/dog/hamster/tortoise did it.

I've never seen it before in my life.

But you said your new stereo/washing machine was so simple even a child could use it.

The television just blew up when I was nowhere near it.

The springs on that sofa were already like that.. It's probably because you're overweight.

But you've always told me you have to turn the gas on for a bit before you light the oven.

When this bloke on the telly balanced a chair on his head it worked.

When that man on the telly did the same thing you laughed and said how funny it was.

They don't make furniture like they used to.

It just fell off the shelf. They must be doing some building work next door.

Oh, *that* chair.

How to get an Adult to take you to a fair/cinema/ for a meal.

But, Mum, you said you were fed up with cooking.

This film is very educational.

Your favourite actor/actress is in this film.

45

This fair is just like the ones when you were small.

All my friends' parents have taken them.

After all, you did say you wanted me out of the house.

How to ~~avoid~~ avoid going somewhere.

(e.g. visiting relatives)

I wouldn't want to be a nuisance to them.

It's such a long way and you know I get car sick.

You'd have a much better time without me there.

When Granny kisses me her moustache brings me out in spots.

You always say you wish you had more time on your own with your Dad/Mum/Sister, etc.

I'm ill and I don't want Gran/Uncle/Aunt to catch it.

HOW TO AVOID GOING TO THE DENTIST.

That dentist took out the wrong tooth of a friend of mine.

Did you know our dentist's an alcoholic?

Did you read about that boy who died when he was given an anaesthetic?

Our dentist cuts himself shaving. Would you allow someone as shaky as that with a drill in your mouth?

I'm allergic to anaesthetic.

I had my teeth checked by the school dentist last week.

I don't want to be a nuisance to the dentist, he's so busy.

How to GET YOUR PARENTS
TO MOVE HOUSE.

You always say the air/climate here is bad for us.

I don't have any friends here.

The price of property is much cheaper in (wherever you want to go).

The schools are much better at (ditto).

(Ditto) is so near Gran/Uncle/the sea/work.

This house is too small for all of us.

Did you know they're going to build a motorway through here?

If we had a bigger house you wouldn't see so much of me.

They reckon property at (your favourite place) will go up by 100% next year.

Have you heard who's moving in next door?

I'd hate to grow old in this house.

The weather at (your favourite place) is wonderful. You'll feel so much better.

The crime rate in this area is increasing. At (your favourite place) they don't have any crime at all.

They're going to make next door into an all-night disco club.

REASONS WHY VIDEO/ARCADE GAMES ARE GOOD FOR YOU.

They improve your reflexes.

You can become famous and rich at them.

They're good practice for later on when I learn to drive/become an airline pilot.

You learn how to handle modern computer technology, which is vitally important for getting a job.

how to get your PARENTS to take you ABROAD ON HOLIDAY.

The price of food and the cost of living is so much cheaper over there.

Air flights abroad are cheaper than travelling in this country by rail or road.

We're guaranteed good weather.

I'm learning to speak that language at school.

We're doing a geography project on that country.

All my friends have been there.

Are we *that* poor that we can't afford it?

A holiday like that will do you good.

Everyone else in my school/the street/the town/ your work/this country has been there.

How To Avoid Having A Haircut.

It keeps me warm. I'll catch cold if it's cut.

The hairdresser/barber suffers from this disease that causes his hands to shake. Last week he cut off a boy's ear.

Everyone else wears their hair like this. You wouldn't want me to look out of place, would you?

My scalp's allergic to the conditioner they use.

The stuff they put on your hair makes it fall out.

Last time they did my hair, they burnt it.

REASONS FOR GOING OUT LATE TO A PARTY OR DISCO.

I said I would be there and you wouldn't want me to let all my friends down, would you?

There's a prize at the disco to see who's the best dancer, and I'm sure I'll win.

I thought I'd go so that you could have some peace and quiet this evening.

My friends say you never allow me out in the evenings, and you wouldn't want them to think that's true.

Your best friend's son/daughter is throwing the party. You wouldn't want them to think I'm being rude by not going, would you?

It's a school disco. My teacher said he/she wanted to meet me there to talk about my school project.

You get a free meal at this party. I thought it would save you the bother of having to cook me something.

There's a raffle at the party and I've already bought some tickets for it. You wouldn't want me to waste my money and miss the chance of winning a prize, would you?

How to get your parents to give you a clothing allowance.

It will teach me to manage my own finances for when I get older.

It will force me to take more care of my clothes.

I'll buy things in fashion instead of you buying me things that everyone laughs at.

I'll start looking around for the cheapest clothes and therefore save money.

You won't have to come shopping with me, so you'll save lots of time.

I'm old enough to handle my own money now.

All my friends have a clothing allowance.

Do you want me to grow up psychologically disturbed because you won't give me the personal freedom of a clothing allowance?

It will save you the strain of worrying what to buy me.

Don't you trust me?

How to get more money for your clothing allowance.

I'm growing so fast that I need to buy clothes more frequently.

Prices have gone up since my clothing allowance began.

How to con money out of adults.

I'm collecting for poor children.

I owe this big bully money and he's threatened to beat me up.

I am saving up to take you out for a slap-up meal.

All that heavy change in your pocket ruins the shape of your clothes. I'll take it off you.

I'm saving up for an adventure holiday so that you can have some time on your own.

I'm doing a sponsored walk/run/silence/swim/collection.

I read in a magazine that dirty, old bank-notes carry germs.

HOW TO GET A PARENT TO STOP ON A LONG CAR JOURNEY.

You don't want me to be sick on the new sheepskin seat covers, do you?

I feel a bit funny. I think it's because I'm hungry.

I'm dying to go to the toilet.

Did you remember to put the petrol cap back on?

I think we've got a petrol leak/slow puncture.

There was a number plate lying on the road back there. It didn't belong to us, did it?

I think I can hear a funny noise coming from the engine.

PUTTING it INTO PRACTICE

In the previous pages, we have outlined practical ways to handle adults. 'Ah!' you scoff, 'that's all right in theory, but what about in practice. Do they work? How do you get away with it? What happens when you come up against really tough grown-ups; grown-ups who are sneaky, devious, and up to all manner of dodges themselves?'

Believe us, our dodges work, and to prove it we are printing extracts from the diary of an arch-dodger friend of ours (who, for obvious reasons, we can only refer to as 'X').

POWER TO KIDS!

KIDS RULE OK!

OR?

HOW TO HANDLE GROWN-UPS

IS PROUD TO PRESENT:

THE DIARY OF X

Sunday 3rd

Auntie Ann came to stay for the day and while she was here insisted on cooking us all a meal. However, as I know how terrible her cooking is, I told her I was on a diet because I was unbelievably overweight. When it came to time for her hideous meal, I told everyone I was just going out for a jog and nipped down to the fish and chip shop.

Monday 4th

Got up. Household in uproar and panic as a result of my secretly putting all the clocks in the house one hour forward last night. Because everyone was rushing around in panic, convinced they were late, I was able to have the best slices of toast and eat two helpings of breakfast without anyone noticing. Took opportunity to ask everyone individually for money for bus fare to school. Everyone paid up, too confused to check with each other.

Tuesday 5th

Bus queue enormous, so I developed pronounced limp as I approached. Considered falling into pitiful heap on pavement to emphasize disability, but thought this might be overdoing it; didn't want to end up being taken to hospital in an ambulance. As it was, sympathetic adults in queue insisted I rest at front to make sure of getting seat on bus. Old lady even gave me her suitcase to sit on while I was waiting – and a couple of toffees!

Wednesday 6th
Problems at school. My lack of science homework has finally come home to roost, purely because my class teacher, Perky Parrott, has started talking to the science teacher, Big-Ears Blunt. (Background note: due to a row over Big-Ears accidentally drinking out of Perky's cup one break-time last term, the two haven't been on speaking terms. I've been able to put this to good use by blaming my lack of science homework on Perky (e.g. 'Mr Parrott took it and said he'd give it to you'; 'Mr Parrott said I was excused all other homework to concentrate on the extra work he's set me', etc. etc.)

Yesterday, drat it, they patched up their row, because Big-Ear's old banger had a puncture and Perky helped him change the wheel. (Perky didn't want to, but he's head of religion and the only one with a jack, so he didn't have much choice.)

The outcome is that I've got to report to the head tomorrow for punishment. Punishment without even a trial! Curses. Wonder what the phone number is of Court of Human Justice at Strasbourg?

Thursday 7th
Do I go to school and take my punishment like a man, or do I stay at home?

Decided to stay at home, it'll give me time to work out escape plan. Went for simplest of all excuses: illness. Used flour to pale face, water to redden eyes, two hot water bottles up jumper to give me a temperature, refused breakfast, and was noisily sick twice. This, added to rumour planted last night of boy in my class with typhoid, led to Mum ordering me to stay in bed. I protested (don't want to arouse suspicion, and it makes grown-ups feel good to score one over you), but she overruled me. Made recovery at 3 p.m. – too late to go to school, but early enough to be able to watch TV this evening ('to take my mind off illness').

Friday 8th
Day of Reckoning
Thanks to yesterday's illness, I had time to prepare my case. Decided 'honest' approach was the answer, grown-ups are helpless against it.

Called in at Twitcher's office (the head), and had fit of nervousness. Admitted guilt, but begged him not to let Perky or Big-Ears beat me. He was shocked at the very idea that I might be beaten, but I hinted that such things went on in their classrooms behind closed doors. (A blatant lie – neither Perky nor Big-Ears could punch their way through a sponge cake, but adults always believe 'there's no smoke without fire' and if they're that stupid, they may as well be encouraged.

On to stage two of the 'honest approach': the shame of being unable to understand the science lessons; Big-Ears' violent temper which terrifies me so much I'm unable to ask for further explanations from him; the awful headaches at the thought of admitting my lack of knowledge; the sleepless nights; the feelings of near-suicide; the relief that it's all 'now out in the open', etc. etc. All the usual garbage.

Twitcher near to tears. Me exonerated. Twitcher to have severe word with Big-Ears. Me excused science homework 'for the time being' (which could mean indefinitely). Wonder if it would work with maths? Probably not, even grown-ups can't be that thick (well, not all of them).

Saturday 9th

Went with family to see Grandad. The journey was so long I told Dad I was going to be sick, thus forcing him to stop the car at the next motorway services. Lost Dad £5 on the fruit machines there.

When we finally arrived Grandad gave me £5 which I pocketed quickly, dead scared Dad would claim it for the money I'd lost on the fruit machines.

Sunday 10th
Stayed in bed.

Monday 11th

I brought up the topic of my birthday present today with my Mum and said that a nice bike (BMX?) would be the best thing because it would save her my bus fare to school and make me more independent. She must have got the message because later on that day when we went out shopping, I saw her looking at prices in a cycle magazine in the newsagents.

Tuesday 12th

This morning I decided my parents weren't giving me enough to eat. So I told Mum I had a friend coming round for dinner and that she had an enormous appetite. Mum agreed to buy lots of extra food when she went shopping to compensate for my friend's visit. Later on, when Mum came back, her bags were absolutely packed full of all my favourite foods.

Sadly, after Mum had prepared the meal, I had to tell her that my friend's father had phoned to say that my friend had had an accident and wouldn't be able to come for dinner. Mum looked dismayed, saying 'Oh no, what on earth shall I do with all this food?' I comforted her by saying that as she had bought it all because of me, it was down to me to dispose of it.

Wednesday 13th

Gran (Mum's Mum) came to stay for an indefinite period. Terrible. She complained to Dad and Mum that they were bringing me up wrongly: 'That child gets away with murder. He's lazy and treats you like servants. He should be made to do some of the work around the house.' Considered putting superglue in her false teeth cleaner to shut her up, but dismissed this as too obvious, I'd be bound to get caught.

Dad and Mum, terrified of her, made me wash up. Immediate 'accident': broke the coronation mug that Gran gave Mum. This got me out of the rest of the washing-up, but Gran insisted I was sent to bed without any supper. This is going to be a tough time. If I hadn't had the foresight to lay in a supply of food from the fridge, I'd be in trouble.

Thursday 14th

More pressure on me (as a result of Gran) to help about the house: wash up, dust, vacuum, clean windows, etc. My standard excuses to get out of such chores (growing pains throughout body; allergy to dust; fear of electrocution by household appliances; breakages, etc.) met a complete stone wall.

Finally I was forced to clean the outsides of the windows. (Shall look up the number of the NSPCC later.) It was the humiliation I couldn't stand, especially when I was spotted by that idiot Mark Thomson from my class. I had to pretend to him it was all part of a ruse, but I was so put out I accidentally broke a window. Any other time this would have been a good dodge, but not so soon after the coronation mug, and not with Gran around.

The end result (suggested by Gran, of course) is that I lose my pocket money until the broken window is paid for. That woman has got to go!

Friday 15th

Decided to use totally different strategy: Operation Be-Nice-To-Grandma. Took Grandma early morning cup of tea in bed. Mum and Dad think I'm wonderful, Gran impressed as well. Gran kept in bathroom for hours by laxative I'd put in her tea. Dad annoyed, unable to get into bathroom. Gran insisted it was 'something she ate' – Mum upset by this slur on her cooking.

I suggested that Mum and Dad call in the doctor to look at Gran. Gran touched by my concern for her.

Saturday 16th

Early morning tea for Gran again (no laxative this time, otherwise she'd get suspicious). While she drank I asked after her health and received a complete list of ailments from migraine in the head to bunions on the feet. That's where all the Health Service money goes! I told her she could count on me to help her. She, touched, said she wished other people in our house showed as much concern.

In an effort to be 'helpful', I thought it a good idea to pass this on to Dad and Mum. Dad rather put out at suggestion that he shows no concern for Gran. Mum says Gran has a point.

Dad not talking to Mum. Mum, still miffed over yesterday's dig at her cooking, not talking to Gran. Their not talking to one another is very useful, as they can't double-check the hints I drop about what each has been saying about the other.

Sunday 17th

Remove colour supplements from Sunday papers as soon as they are delivered, and leave them in Gran's room. Deny all knowledge when asked if I've seen them.

Mum finds them four hours later. Gran claims Dad must have left them there, 'He's always been one for leaving things lying around.'

Decided now was a good time to increase pressure: added extra salt to Mum's Sunday dinner. Dad silent on subject (from bitter experience). Gran complained volubly. Mum peeved at Gran.

Monday 18th

Stuck hairs from Dad's shaving brush on bar of Gran's special soap in bathroom. Furious row.

Atmosphere too hostile for anyone to notice me, except to use me as confidant to complain about the others. (Gone are the days of ordering me to wash up.)

Gran sees me as her only friend in this house, tells me she plans to cut Dad and Mum out of her will and leave everything to me. I murmur 'No you shouldn't', but wonder how I can find out how much she's got?

Tuesday 19th

Boy next door called in for few minutes. I blamed him for the whoopee cushion on Gran's chair. (As expected, due to tension between them, Dad fell about as Gran sat on whoopee cushion.) Gran furious.

Gran left.

Later admitted to Dad and Mum separately that I was the culprit. As expected, they were both grateful. Both complimented me on my honesty, and both gave me a pound.

Wednesday 20th
Discussion at school on future careers. Perky Parrott said with my talents I was ideally suited to politics. From what I've heard about politicians, he could be right.

The end

2. WHAT GROWN-UPS SAY & WHAT THEY REALLY MEAN

WHY YOU NEED THIS book

Grown-ups are liars. They lie to children, and they are convinced that children believe them.

For example, when a child asks a grown-up for something, or to go out somewhere, the adult won't say 'No' directly, even though he/she wants to. Instead the adult will say things like:

We'll talk about it later.

You'll have to ask your father/mother.

Wait and see.

I'll have to think about it.

I might.

Things are a bit difficult at the moment.

Are you sure it's what you really want/want to do?

When grown-ups want to avoid answering awkward questions, they say:

Now is not the time to discuss this.

I'm in the middle of reading/ironing/watching TV/scratching my nose.

Talk it over with your mother/father.

I didn't think you were interested in that.

We'll talk about it later.

I've got a sore throat, I can't talk.

Is it *really* important?

I'll have to think about that.

Why do they do this? Because they want to be thought of as 'nice' by everybody, including children. Well this is where we blow the gaff! Read this book and find out 'What Grown-Ups Say . . . (AND WHAT THEY REALLY MEAN!)'

POWER TO KIDS!

KIDS RULE OK!

OR?

AT HOME

Nobody cares about me. I cook, wash, and clean for the whole family, and I get nothing in return. Be a dear and wash up for me. After all, I know you care about me, you're different from the others. You don't want me to get ill, do you. *(Wash up and you'll get in my good books. If you don't I'll make you feel guilty.)*

What's this lying on the floor? *(I know jolly well what it is, but I want you to pick it up.)*

I want to have a serious talk with you. *(I'm going to tell you off.)*

It will do you good to have an early night tonight. *(I want you out of my way this evening.)*

You've had that shirt a long time. It's too small/too big for you. *(Don't wear that shirt, I don't like it.)*

Where were you this evening? *(I know where you were but I want to make you feel guilty for not telling me/coming home late.)*

How did you get on at school today, dear? *(I'm not the slightest bit interested, I'm only asking to be polite.)*

Your friend has a very interesting character. *(I don't like him/her.)*

Would you like to go on an adventure holiday? *(I'd really like to get you out of my way for a bit.)*

That TV programme you're watching doesn't look very interesting. *(Turn that telly off.)*

Nobody seems to take responsibility for the work in the kitchen. *(Do some housework.)*

How are you getting on with your homework? *(Hurry up and do your homework.)*

It's getting late. *(Go to bed.)*

That book you're reading doesn't seem very exciting/important for your education. *(I don't approve of that book, read something else.)*

You were late back from school today, dear. *(Why were you late back from school?)*

You're getting much too old for that childish little personal stereo of yours. *(I want that, give it to me.)*

If you were a girl/boy you wouldn't do that. *(I wish you were a girl/boy.)*

Your friend is quite nice really. *(Your friend is really horrible.)*

Nature hasn't looked too kindly on your friend, has it. *(Your friend is really ugly.)*

I suppose your friend's parents had difficulty in bringing him/her up. *(He/she is a right thug.)*

Don't forget, the doctor said because of your sore throat you mustn't use your voice too much. *(Shut up.)*

We've decided we aren't getting enough exercise, so we're going to do more walking, cycling etc., and we won't be needing the car any more. *(We're going to have to sell the car.)*

Your mother/father and I have decided we've been bringing you up wrongly by spoiling you too much. *(We're so poor we can't afford to treat you any more.)*

I think you ought to get a light part-time job like a paper round to give you practice at earning a living. *(I can't afford to give you pocket money any more.)*

I have a suspicion that you're allergic to chocolate. *(I can't afford to buy you any more sweets.)*

I heard on the news that computers/video games are bad for your health. They can cause headaches and backaches, and a survey showed that 80% of people who play video games suffer from stress. *(If you think I'm buying you a computer/video game you're mistaken!)*

You're much too old for a silly little bike like that, you need something more practical. *(I'm not buying you an expensive bike like that.)*

We're having some friends round for tea today, and I don't really think you'd find them very interesting, so I've arranged for you to go and see your friend. *(I'd feel embarrassed and ashamed if my friends saw your behaviour.)*

Those shoes you wear must be awfully bad for your feet, and as I care so much for your health I worry that they might cause you permanent damage. *(Don't wear those shoes, I feel embarrassed when people see you wearing them.)*

We've been thinking that it might not be a good idea to go on holiday abroad this year. With so many wars going on in foreign countries it's just too dangerous. *(We can't afford to go abroad this year.)*

I'm afraid Mummy/Daddy forgot to renew our passports, and they expired last month. We've sent away for them, but apparently the process takes months. *(We can't afford to go abroad this year.)*

It's time you learnt to do practical things, because there will come a time when I won't be around to do things for you. *(Wash up.)*

Oh dear, this cough of mine is getting worse. Go to the chemist and get me some cough medicine. Oh, and while you're there get. . . . *(Go and do the shopping.)*

Have you tidied your bedroom yet? *(I know you haven't tidied your bedroom. Go and do it.)*

This is for your own good. *(This isn't going to do you any good at all, but it eases my conscience to say it.)*

Do you really feel comfortable in that outfit? *(I'm not going out with you dressed like that!)*

Your bedroom is in an awful mess and I've got Auntie coming to stay and you wouldn't want her to get the wrong impression of you, would you? *(I'd feel ashamed if she saw your room. It would reflect badly on me as a parent.)*

Eat your dinner and you'll grow up big and strong like me. *(This doesn't mean a thing. I just want you to eat your dinner.)*

This soup has got lots of protein in it. *(This soup doesn't have any protein in it, but my mum/dad said it to me and made me eat it, so I'll say it to you.)*

I've been thinking that it would be nice to buy you something more expensive than usual for a present this year, and as your birthday is so near Christmas we could combine the two and give you one big present. *(I can't afford to buy you two separate presents this year.)*

It's much too hot to wear that jumper. *(Don't wear that jumper, you look silly in it.)*

I need to buy some food for us to live on, but I'm a little hard up, and if you want to eat you'd better lend me some money from your savings bank. *(I need some cash off you.)*

Your father/mother and I have decided it would be better for your sake if we lived apart. *(We're splitting up.)*

I've decided that you and daddy/mummy can manage quite well on your own and in many ways you'll be better off without me, so I shall be going away for a while. *(I'm off!)*

You should think yourself lucky, when I was your age I only got sixpence a week pocket money. *(I'm telling you this to make you feel you're getting a lot of money, but I'm hoping you won't twig that that was thirty years ago, and sixpence was a lot then.)*

You've been misbehaving so much lately I think I need to stop your pocket money until you've thought your behaviour over a bit. *(I need more money and this is as good an excuse as any to get it.)*

I do understand that each individual is entitled to his/her own point of view, but I think it's important that you respect and listen to mine. After all, you're only a child and you still aren't aware of all the facts. *(You're going to agree with me whether you like it or not.)*

Do you know there's a huge fair and carnival coming to our town this summer, and I know you'd just love to go. *(We're not going on holiday this year.)*

I don't think you should watch the television so much, it's bad for your eyes. *(I want to watch something else.)*

I wish you would model yourself on your friend. *(I much prefer him/her to you.)*

Dyeing your hair is very bad for it. It might even make it fall out. *(I feel embarrassed when you dye your hair.)*

Why don't you get the paperback version. After all, you might tear it, then all that money would be wasted. *(I'm not buying you a book that expensive!)*

Has your piano teacher made any comment on your progress? *(Stop making that dreadful row on that piano!)*

You were such a beautiful sweet darling when you were younger. *(You're getting really ugly.)*

Have you thought of taking an interest in classical music? *(I can't stand that awful rubbish you keep playing.)*

It would be unfair of me to put the responsibility of looking after it on your young shoulders. *(I wouldn't trust a clumsy twit like you with it.)*

That's all right, you can go out and have fun. I don't mind staying in on my own. *(You're not going out, because if you do I'll make you feel guilty.)*

It's surprising how you almost forget birthdays as you get older. *(It's my birthday next week. Don't forget it.)*

I do wish you wouldn't keep phoning your friends all the time. Everybody finds it very irritating with you hogging the phone constantly. *(Stop bumping up my phone bill with all your calls.)*

Your school report says you're not doing too well at English, so I think you should get some practice by writing to your friends instead of phoning them. *(I can't afford your being on the phone all the time.)*

I sometimes think I let you have things your own way too often. *(You're spoilt, and I'm going to be tough on you.)*

My, how you've grown! *(God, I'm getting old.)*

You *have* changed since I last saw you. *(Who the hell are you?)*

He certainly takes after his father. *(What an ugly child.)*

Do you want me to help you with your homework? *(I want to feel useful and impress you.)*

Ssssh, I'm thinking. *(I'm tired and I want to sleep.)*

I wish you'd be more like your father/mother. *(I can control your father/mother.)*

I don't know. *(I know but I'm not telling you.)*

I know but I'm not telling you. *(I don't know.)*

I know the answers to all those questions, but I think it's important that you find out for yourself. *(I haven't a clue.)*

When I was your age I respected adults. *(I did no such thing, but I wish you'd respect me.)*

I deliberately didn't give you any help with your Maths homework because I feel it is important that you work those sums out for yourself. *(I haven't a clue how to do them.)*

How long have you been wearing that shirt/jumper/those trousers. *(Change them, they're filthy.)*

Thank you, dear, it's just what I wanted. *(Ugh, how can I get rid of it tactfully.)*

Did you make it yourself? *(What on earth is it?)*

When did you last wash your hands? *(Go and wash your hands.)*

I sometimes wonder if I'm a bad influence on you. *(Tell me how wonderful I am.)*

I'm concerned for your health. I think you're watching far too much TV, so I'm moving it into my room. *(I'm going to have the telly all to myself from now on so I can watch what I want to.)*

I think those comics you read are having a bad effect on your education. *(I'm not buying you any more of those rubbishy comics.)*

What do you think of my new dress/suit/hairstyle? *(Tell me how good I look.)*

When did you last wash/have a bath/shower? *(I know when it was. I want you to wash/bath now.)*

How are you enjoying school? *(I can't think what to talk about to children.)*

OUT AND ABOUT

Let's take the car into town, it's too dangerous to walk/cycle. *(I'm not fit enough to walk/cycle all that way.)*

I don't think that kind of garment suits you very well, and, besides, they'll be out of fashion in a couple of months. *(I can't afford to buy you expensive clothes like that.)*

Well personally I wouldn't choose that kind of thing, but you're entitled to your own opinion. However, I'm going to ask you to consider something else. *(I don't like that so you're not getting it.)*

We can't stop at the service station because it will make us late. *(I'm not having you wasting my money on video games/junk food.)*

Don't you think Uncle's new house is wonderful? *(I know it's a dump but say it's wonderful to be polite.)*

I do wish you'd eat a little more slowly. You'll get terrible indigestion if you don't, and also you're liable to spoil your food if you eat with your mouth open. *(Eat properly, you're embarrassing me.)*

I'm trying very hard to concentrate on driving and I find it very distracting when you keep mentioning things. *(Shut up.)*

It's just around the corner. *(It's at least another two miles.)*

This is educational. *(Stop fidgeting, I like museums/art galleries.)*

I loved museums when I was your age. *(I've got a bad memory.)*

Do you have to do that? *(Stop it, you're showing me up.)*

Over-eating is bad for you. *(I'm not buying you a big meal.)*

Let's not stop here, there might be a nicer place further on. *(We're not stopping anywhere if I can help it.)*

You don't have to eat it all if you can't finish it. *(Hurry up and finish your meal, I want some of it.)*

Do you want all your potatoes/meat/pudding? *(I want some.)*

You didn't have to come shopping with me. *(You did have to come shopping with me, and stop complaining.)*

Would you like to go on ahead? *(I'm not walking along with you looking like that.)*

I would like to get you a nice big stereo like that, but the problem is the walls are too thin and we'd have the neighbours complaining all the time. *(A big stereo would cost too much.)*

I don't think there is any point in me getting you nice clothes like that because you're still growing very fast and they wouldn't fit you after a month or two. *(Those clothes are too expensive.)*

As I've put myself out to bring you here today you might at least show some interest. *(I know this bores you but I wanted to come here.)*

I'm not going to support you in damaging your eyesight on those awful arcade games while we're here. *(I'm not giving you any money to play them with.)*

The speedo needle rattles between 40mph and 100mph and it drives me crazy, and I can't exactly crawl along the motorway doing less than 40, can I. *(I love driving fast.)*

I read in a magazine that a car becomes much more economical when driven over 70mph. *(I want to outrun the Ferrari coming up behind us.)*

It's much cheaper for us to travel by coach because our car isn't very economical. *(The car wouldn't start.)*

I thought it would be better for us to travel by train, you see so much more that way. *(Our car is a wreck, but I'm too proud to admit it.)*

I'm not travelling any faster because I consider it would be putting you in danger. *(I'm not going any faster because I haven't got the guts.)*

I'm not going any faster because this road is too bendy. *(My car won't go any faster.)*

That whining noise is just the wind. *(It's actually the engine, but I'm hoping you won't realize it.)*

I really don't think you'd like the food they cook in there. *(I can't afford to take you to a place like that.)*

I think we should wait until that film comes out on video, then we can see it in a far more relaxed atmosphere. *(I'm not taking you to see it.)*

I don't think you'd like this film I'm going to see. In fact it's not your sort of film at all so I've arranged for you to go and stay with a friend of yours for the evening. *(I want an evening at the pictures without you around.)*

Pop-corn/ice-cream/sweets is/are bad for you. *(I'm too mean to buy you any.)*

All the reviews I read of that film are pretty bad. *(I want to go and see another film, and as I'm paying that's the film we're going to see.)*

When I was young we made our own entertainments. *(I'm not giving you any money for video games.)*

We won't eat there, it looks very unhygienic and I'm sure the food will be terrible. *(It looks too expensive.)*

That popcorn you're eating is stopping me from hearing the film. I'll look after it and give it back to you after the film. *(I want to eat it.)*

We're not eating there, it doesn't look to me as if the food is very good value for money. (*It definitely looks too expensive.*)

I find it very irritating when you crunch popcorn all the way through a film. It spoils my enjoyment. (*I'm not buying you anything to eat.*)

He/she has been so looking forward to visiting his/her Gran/Aunt/Uncle, haven't you dear. (*Say 'Yes' and smile when you say it, or you'll be in big trouble when you get home.*)

Oh dear, I've run out of money. Lend me some until we get home. (*And that's the last you'll see of it.*)

I used to carry the heavy shopping for my mother. (*Carry the shopping.*)

While we're out I want you to be on your best behaviour so that people can see what a nice person you really are. (*Please don't show me up.*)

I'm only telling you for your own good. (*Your behaviour reflects on me as a parent.*)

Would you go and browse/look over there for a minute. I want to have a private word with your mother/father. (*We're going to have a row.*)

When I was your age I loved going for long walks. (*I want to go for a walk, no one else wants to come with me, so I'm going to make you accompany me. I'm your parent and you'll do as I tell you.)*

I think we ought to spend more time looking at our surroundings, instead of just rushing along. I suggest we sit down for a minute and admire the view. *(I'm worn out, but I'm too proud to admit it.)*

I don't think you appreciate the time, effort and money I've put into bringing you up. *(No, you can't have that radio/record/jacket/whatever.)*

SChooL
reports

GENERAL COMMENTS

Works well in class. *(Never in class.)*

A popular child. *(The school bully.)*

A good all-round worker. *(Useless at everything.)*

Shows great wit. *(Rude and insolent.)*

Shows an interest. *(But not in the school or any subjects.)*

Responds to a structured environment. *(Needs locking up.)*

I wish more pupils had his/her attitude to school *(and stayed away as often)*.

We hope he/she will go far. *(We wish you would move to another district.)*

A lively child. *(A pain in the neck.)*

Lacks confidence in his/her own ability *(and quite rightly)*.

A very individual achievement this year. *(Bottom of the class.)*

Needs lots of individual help. *(Are we sure this child is human?)*

A questioning mind. *(A troublemaker.)*

A leading figure in class discussions. *(Talks all the time.)*

Shows initiative. *(A thief.)*

Needs lots of attention. *(Ought to be kept tied up.)*

A valuable member of the class. *(Who is this child? I've never seen him/her before in my life.)*

Takes his/her opportunities. *(Takes anything if it isn't nailed down.)*

Has talent. *(But we haven't the faintest idea what in.)*

An example to the rest of the school. *(A bad example.)*

Tries hard. *(And keeps failing.)*

A forceful personality. *(A bully.)*

Very keen. *(Can't wait to get out of school when the bell goes.)*

A promising pupil. *(Always promising to work, never does.)*

A sensitive child. *(A vicious unspeakably nasty piece of work with psychopathic tendencies, liable to erupt into violence if things do not go his/her way)* or *(A wimp)*.

Works hard. *(Achieves nothing.)*

With a little more effort he/she could achieve a good result. *(The lazy twit does absolutely nothing.)*

Achieved expected result in end of term exam. *(0 out of 100.)*

Has greatly improved this term. *(He/she couldn't have got any worse.)*

A good average member of the class. *(Don't know this child.)*

Has great potential. *(Never does any work.)*

He/she prefers outdoor activities. *(Plays truant.)*

An interesting personality. *(This child is dangerous!)*

Has trouble concentrating. *(Thick as a brick.)*

Could try harder. *(Never does anything.)*

His/her attention wanders easily. *(Ditto.)*

His/her achievement doesn't match his/her effort. *(Yes it does – nought effort, nought achievement.)*

ENGLISH

Spelling presents no problem. *(Because we can't understand his/her writing.)*

Shows an interest in books. *(Tears them up.)*

Is more proficient at reading than writing. *(Illiterate.)*

Writing presents some problems. *(Unable to take lid off pen without assistance.)*

A flair for creative writing. *(A liar.)*

Interested in literature. *(Steals books from library.)*

His/her best achievement is in oral work. *(Can't read, can't write, talks all the time.)*

Imaginative use of words. *(Foul-mouthed.)*

PHYSICS

Has an interesting future in electronics. *(Ought to be electrocuted.)*

Seems happy with this subject. *(Thick as a brick, but always smiling.)*

HISTORY

Has expressed an interest in history. *(Asked where he/she should have been yesterday.)*

. Has stated that history is his/her favourite subject. *(Pity it's not shown in his/her work.)*

Has a good head for dates. *(Looks like a date.)*

Good exam result. *(Cheated.)*

RELIGION

Whenever I think of this child, I autortically relate him/her to this subject. *(Oh God!)*

MATHS

Has average ability for his/her group. *(The rest of the group are in the monkey cage at the zoo.)*

Advanced maths causes some problems. *(Has to take shoes off to count higher than 10.)*

Brain suited to geometry. *(A blockhead.)*

Has made some progress. *(Turns up for lessons now.)*

Has shown more interest in maths this year. *(Stayed awake in class more often.)*

GEOGRAPHY

Has problems with geography. *(Doesn't even know where he/she is half the time, let alone where the rest of the world is.)*

Seems comfortable with an atlas. *(Sleeps on it in lesson time.)*

GAMES

Useful in team games. *(Should be used as a goal post.)*

Sports are his/her favourite subject. *(Thick as a plank.)*

Has represented the school at both football and cricket. *(There are only eleven boys in the school.)*

CHEMISTRY

A keen interest in practical work. *(Blew up the laboratory on purpose.)*

LANGUAGES

Works hard at languages. *(But still having trouble with English.)*

Foreign languages will present no problems. *(Providing he/she never leaves the country.)*

WOODWORK

Has a great sympathy with the subject. *(Head like a plank of wood.)*

Has produced a great deal of work. *(Three bags of sawdust.)*

ART AND CRAFT

Made some progress with drawing. *(Has learnt to hold a pencil with the pointed end downwards.)*

Imaginative and unconventional approach. *(Draws on walls.)*

Has a basic knowledge of art. *(Able to get lids off paints.)*

An unusual artistic vision. *(Incompetent.)*

Immerses himself/herself in the subject. *(Gets covered in clay and paint.)*

RURAL STUDIES

Interested in plant life. *(Eats vegetables.)*

Has a future in Rural Studies. *(Would make a good plough.)*

At home in this subject. *(Brain like a cow.)*

MUSIC

Has a good ear. *(The rest of him/her is rotten.)*

Could have a future in music. *(Good at moving pianos.)*

An interesting ear for music. *(Tone deaf.)*

BIOLOGY

Some achievement in this subject. *(Knows what a person looks like.)*

COMPUTER STUDIES

Has a good grasp of the subject. *(Plays video games.)*

DOMESTIC SCIENCE

Achieved a great deal in cookery. *(Eats everything.)*

BOTANY

Is not really equal to the subject. *(Less intelligent than a plant.)*

POLITICAL SCIENCE

This subject is well suited to his/her talents. *(This child is devious, shifty, and not to be trusted.)*

TECHNICAL DRAWING

Produced some interesting work this year.
(Haven't the faintest idea what it was.)

I insist on absolute silence in my classroom. (*I prefer the sound of my own voice.*)

That child there, stop doing that or I shall report you! (*I can't report you because I don't know who you are.*)

This is Mr/Mrs Bloggs, who's kindly come to talk to you about his adventures as a carpet salesman in Birmingham/her life mending shoes in Bournemouth, which will be of great interest to you. (*I've fixed this so I can get two hours off.*)

You think you can get away with this, do you? (*You know you can get away with this.*)

I didn't behave that way when I was at school. (*I behaved just like that when I was at school.*)

Right, you, what's the answer? (*You obviously weren't paying attention and didn't hear the question, so I'm going to show you up in front of everybody.*)

No one in my class would do a thing like that. (*Of course someone in my class did that, but if I admit it it will reflect badly on me as a teacher.*)

Now although this is a Cup match, I want you to play a good clean game. (Win at all costs, my reputation as a sports teacher depends on it.)

Unless the culprit owns up I shall keep the whole class in after school. *(Please, please own up or I shall have to admit that I can't keep everyone in after all.)*

Unfortunately I shan't be in tomorrow. *(Hurrah, a break from you lot!)*

This exam is very important. *(This exam is meaningless, I just want to make you work hard.)*

If anyone else misbehaves I shall send for the Head. *(No I won't, because it will mean admitting I can't control a class.)*

When the whistle blows I want everyone standing ABSOLUTELY STILL. *(When the whistle blows just carry on as you always do.)*

Now when the visitors come round I want them to have a good impression of you, so let's see everyone hard at work. *(When the visitors come round I want them to have a good impression of me as a teacher.)*

I've never known such a badly-behaved class. *(Every class I take is as badly behaved.)*

I want you to achieve some good exam results. *(My promotion depends on it.)*

Team, I want you to make the school proud of you. *(Make the head teacher pleased with me for training you.)*

I will not tolerate this kind of behaviour any longer! *(I give up.)*

If you do that again you'll be in serious trouble. *(If you do that again I don't know what I'm going to do about it.)*

I won't tell you again. *(I will tell you again, and again, and again, and you probably won't take any notice of me.)*

I shall ignore that rude noise. Whoever did it is beneath contempt. *(I don't know who did it, and if I try to find out we'll be here for ever and then you'll get out of doing any work. Teaching you lot is like banging my head against a wall.)*

Right, just for that the whole class will sit up straight and remain in silence for the rest of the lesson. *(Great, I didn't have a lesson prepared anyway and now I can have a few minutes' peace.)*

I want you to check your work very carefully because I shall be going through it with a fine toothcomb – woe betide anyone if there are mistakes! *(I shan't even bother to read it, I'll just put a tick at the bottom of every page, and then a big tick at the end.)*

Because you've all worked so hard I'm going to let you off homework tonight. *(I don't feel like doing any marking.)*

I shall be in a meeting in the staff room this lunchtime and we don't want to be disturbed, so I don't want anyone knocking on the door asking for me. *(I'm going to have a sleep at lunchtime.)*

I do know who committed this offence, but I want that person to own up of their own accord. *(I haven't the faintest idea who did it.)*

130

On this school trip you will be representing the school, so I know you will all be on your best behaviour. (*I'm scared stiff you're all going to behave appallingly so I'm appealing to your better natures.*)

What we're going to do today in Maths/Science/Geography/etc. is revise and consolidate the work that we've done so far. (*I haven't planned a lesson for today.*)

It's about time you lot learnt some self-discipline, so today you're going to practise being quiet. (*I've got a hangover.*)

School dinners are balanced to give you proper nutrition. (*The school cook should be shot.*)

I don't want anyone else annoying the school caretaker. Be more considerate of him – he has a hard job to do. (*The school caretaker really runs this school, and he can get me sacked. Be more considerate of me.*)

When I was at school I was captivated by Shakespeare. (*I wasn't allowed to get out of reading him either, and like you lot I couldn't understand a word, but since I had to suffer him now you're going to.*)

Everyone here should be able to do these sums with ease. (*Especially me, because I've got the answers.*)

If you're not sure what to do, just ask me. *(And I will tell you to go away and work it out for yourself.)*

Well, this is the last day of the school year, and I would like to say how much I've enjoyed teaching you all. *(Unfortunately I can't. You lot are the worst rabble since Genghis Khan and his mob.)*

I've worked very hard to improve your standard of education, but . . . *(I've done nothing, you've done nothing. Was it worth us even turning up?)*

Do you think I enjoy telling you off all the time? *(I do, actually. It gives me a feeling of power.)*

how to delibeRATElY

mISUNDERSTAND

ADULTs

double-talk

AN ADULT

When an adult asks you 'What's that on the floor?' (meaning 'Pick that up'), be very 'helpful' and answer their question: 'It looks like a piece of paper – or it could be a piece of fluff. Hang on, it's a drop of porridge. . . . No, no, it's . . . I'm not really sure. Have you got any ideas?'

By this time the adult in question will be having a nervous breakdown. Try this trick a few times and you will soon have your adults well trained: they will pick the thing up for themselves, rather than go through it all. The alternative is for them to order you to pick the thing up – and if they do you can counter-attack with, 'But I didn't drop it. . . .' This can develop into an investigation of who did drop it, and by the time they've discovered that it really was you after all, the dog will have eaten whatever it was.

To explain what I mean in greater detail, here are some examples from my infamous 'Diary of X', showing how I dealt with grown-ups who tried it on me. . . .

What grown-
ups
say
and what they really
MEAN
is proud to present
THE
DIARY of
X

137

Friday 13th

A suitable date for today's entry. A truly terrible day. Today I am being turned out of my home by my unfeeling parents. Ah well, it had to happen. I suppose it must be hard for them to live with a genius like me. I fought against it, of course, but for once I lost.

It came like a bombshell yesterday at breakfast. I'd just started on my second helping of cornflakes (the last lot in the packet, but I'd persuaded Dad that he was getting fat), when Dad said, 'Your mother and I think you're looking under the weather, and that a couple of weeks by the sea would do you good.'

Well, I was delighted. All those hints I'd dropped about underprivileged children who never go on holiday had finally worked. Then came the bombshell: 'So we've arranged with your Uncle Steve and your Auntie Sheila for you to stay with them for the next two weeks.'

I nearly choked on my cornflakes. Uncle Steve and Auntie Sheila are two of the most mindless people ever invented. They're an ageing hippie couple who live on a marsh somewhere on the East Coast, where the land is so flat they have to tie the grass down to stop it blowing away.

It is a truly terrible part of the universe, and Uncle Steve and Auntie Sheila are two really zapped-out idiots, who wander round simpering

at people and going 'Peace and love'. If anything
upsets them they say things like, 'Man, this is
too heavy for me,' and 'We should communicate
with the universe more.' In short, they are
wimps calculated to drive any sane person to
banging his/her head against a wall.

They don't believe in video games, they don't
believe in pop radio, and they only have a television for Uncle Steve's Open University
Course.

'Uncle Steve and Auntie Sheila?' I croaked,
aghast.

'We thought you'd be pleased,' said Dad.

'And it will do you good,' said Mum.

At first I was too stunned even to object – how
could they do this to me? And then I started:

1. The damp marsh climate would bring on rheumatism, asthma, flu, pneumonia, the plague.
2. Being miles from anywhere would lead me to become a lost and lonely child.
3. Uncle Steve and Auntie Sheila weren't near the sea. No one on that part of the East Coast was near the sea because there were mud-flats a hundred miles wide between the marshes and the sea. I would disappear in the mud-flats and never be seen again.
4. Uncle Steve and Auntie Sheila were peculiar and their hippie life-style would lead me astray.
5. I wanted to stay near the parents I loved (Sob).

Etc. etc. etc. and so on. All to no avail.

In short, what Dad and Mum were saying when they said 'We think you're under the weather and that a couple of weeks by the sea will do you good,' was: 'We can stand you no longer. If we could we would tie a heavy weight around your neck and drop you in the canal, but failing that we are going to inflict you on Steve and Sheila. We will then be free of you for two weeks, and maybe suffering their wimp-like life-style will make you appreciate us more, and toe the line when you get back.'

All was lost. It was with a heavy heart that I went down to the video arcade. It was no consolation playing on Dad and Mum's feelings of guilt, and conning them both (separately) out of a pound to play the games – or even conning the arcade manager into letting me have a free game after I'd 'lost' a non-existent coin in the slot.

I was doomed to go to Steve and Sheila's.

Saturday 14th
Today I was dumped on the lunatic fringe of the family (Steve is Dad's brother).

All my last-minute efforts to get a reprieve were to no avail: racking coughs, stomach pains, suspected leprosy, dizziness, home-sickness, travel-sickness, all came to nothing. Even my appeal to my mother as I handed her my old bus pass ('Take this. If anything should happen to me while I'm away, look at it and remember me') had no effect. How hard-hearted they are. (*Mental memo:* while I'm away I shall make an anonymous phone call to the police and tell them my disappearance is due to being murdered, and my body is buried in my dad's favourite flower-bed. When his begonias are dug up by hundreds of coppers he'll regret sending me away.)

Steve and Sheila met me at the station with their usual wimp-like niceties: 'Hey, how wonderful to see you again. It's going to be fun having you around.' (*Translation:* 'We didn't want you to come here, but we couldn't get out of it because we owe your parents too many favours.')

I smiled politely and let them show me the view as they drove me back to their hovel in the middle of the marsh: 'Look at the scenery. You can see for miles.' (*Translation:* 'This is the flattest, most boring piece of country in the world but it's cheap because no one in their right mind would want to live here.')

142

When we arrived back at their place – 'It's not very plush but it's our kind of house.' (*Translation:* It's a dump because we can't be bothered to do anything to it, like sweep up) – Sheila suggested that I must be tired after my long journey, and maybe I'd like to have an early night. (*Translation:* 'Let's get this kid out of our way at the earliest opportunity.')

I countered by saying that I had been so looking forward to seeing them again that I would rather spend my first evening in their company. The sight of their faces falling was a joy to my heart.

Our first evening was the ultimate in boredom: they read books and listened to Radio 3. This was too much for me and I decided to give them the First Round, and went to bed.

A plan is forming in my brain. These two weeks could be fun after all. I am going to take on Uncle Steve and Aunt Sheila and stir them up. They have always been so laid-back and wimplike, pretending to be so 'caring', that I'm determined to make them crack and give vent to their real feelings.

I am going to force them to stop lying when they say things, and get them to say what they really mean.

Yes, these two weeks could be fun.

Sunday 15th
Into the attack today. Got off to a flying start when Uncle Steve was showing me some of his wood carvings.

'Of course,' he said with lots of false modesty, 'they're not really very good.'

It was his way of saying they *were* very good, and getting me to agree, and say, 'Oh, really, they're wonderful', or some such guff. Instead I nodded sympathetically and said, 'Not to worry, I'm sure lots of other people find wood carving just as difficult as you do.'

This threw him, so he added rather pointedly: 'Of course, Sheila thinks they're very good and says I ought to exhibit them.'

I just smiled sympathetically and said nothing. That rattled him.

Monday 16th
Shopping with Aunt Sheila today.

Standing in the shop, she said, 'I'll carry this big heavy shopping bag back to the car.'

(*Translation:* 'This shopping is too heavy for me, so would you carry it? I'd ask you directly, but I don't want to be thought of as a bossy adult.')

I was supposed to reply, 'No no, Auntie, *I'll* carry that one.' Instead I said, 'Very well, Auntie, if you'd prefer it that way,' picked up the little bag, and carried that back to the car.

The big bag was so heavy Aunt Sheila's put her back out. That'll teach her.

Tuesday 17th
Think I'm getting through to Uncle and Auntie. Caught them glaring at me today, though they broke into happy smiles when they saw me looking at them. They also came up with, 'We thought it would be nice for you to get the feel of

145

the country around here without us hanging around you today.' *(Translation:* 'Keep out of our sight today.')* I countered with: 'No no, my pleasure is in your company.' That wiped the smiles from their faces.

Wednesday 18th
The swines! They've made a really vicious move against me: they've got rid of the telly! They said, 'We thought while you were here we'd lock away the television. After all, it gets in the way of conversation, and you said you preferred the pleasure of our company. As you feel that way, we thought it was the least we could do.' *(Translation:* 'We've hidden the telly. *That'll* force you to leave.')* The swines.

Thursday 19th
Found the telly today. The crafty pair had hidden it in their bedroom, under a cloth.

Used ruse to get it back into the living room: I told them that the late film on the telly was of a book we were doing at school, and our English teacher had told us all to watch it. I asked if I could join them in their bedroom for this special occasion and watch the film on the telly. As I expected, under the threat of me invading their private room, the telly reappeared.

Rather than take a chance on it being removed again, I put superglue on the television table, so it stuck when they put it down.

A close shave. Do not underestimate these people.

Friday 20th

A classic line from Aunt Sheila today: 'We thought you might be feeling guilty about not helping around the house, so we've made a list of jobs for you, to make you feel more comfortable.' (*Translation:* 'We're sick of seeing you do nothing but laze around, so we're going to make you work.')

This was easily dealt with by doing the jobs wrong (broke the axe while chopping wood; broke two plates and a cup while washing up; fed the dog too much dog food, with the result it was sick all over the carpet.)

All in all, a successful day.

Saturday 21st

Uncle Steve and Aunt Sheila's patience definitely wearing thin. Their smiles are now starting to look a little stretched, and they're starting to snarl a bit. Today Uncle Steve's 'caring' manner slipped. It started with him giving me a friendly: 'I bet you can't run down to the post box and back in three minutes.' (*Translation:* 'Post this letter for me.')

I said: 'You're right, I can't. I'm no good at athletics.'

He tried again with: 'Haven't you got a letter to post to your parents?' I said: 'No, they said there was no need to write to them.'

At this his cool slipped and he snapped: 'Take this letter to the post box, you crafty little. . . .' I immediately expressed 'surprise', and said

sadly, 'I'm sorry, Uncle Steve, I didn't realize you wanted me to run an errand for you, or I would have offered with pleasure.'

This caused a right royal row. As I was leaving the house with the letter, I could hear Aunt Sheila telling Uncle Steve off for being so unkind and raising his voice to me; and Uncle Steve telling her if she thought I was really so innocent then she had the brain of a paralyzed chicken.

Another one to me.

Sunday 22nd
Day off. Stayed in bed.

Monday 23rd
The swines got me again!

This morning they said, 'We're going to a talk on yak acupuncture in Tibet this afternoon. We know you'll be bored by it and you'd prefer to have the afternoon on your own.' This was such an unsubtle way of saying, 'We're going off on our own to get away from you this afternoon,' that I nearly laughed out loud. However, keeping to my discipline of losing no chance to call their bluff, I said: 'Oh no, I'd love to go with you. Yak acupuncture fascinates me.'

So I went with them . . . and they really did take me to a three-hour talk on yak acupuncture. The swines! Three hours of sitting in a draughty hall watching some bloke show slides of pins sticking in a yak's foot.

They'll pay for this!

Tuesday 24th

Tonight Steve and Sheila threw a dinner party.

Actually it wasn't the *party* that should have been thrown, it was the food. Seaweed fritters. Burgers made out of grass.

The place was full of people with head-bands on, being patronizing to me and saying things like, 'I really relate to kids.' (*Translation:* 'I have a mental age of four'); 'What are you going to do when you leave school?' (*Translation:* 'I haven't the faintest idea what to talk to children about, so I'll lead the conversation towards talking about adult work'); and 'Childhood is such a precious time of life.' (*Translation:* 'I'm glad I'm not a kid any more.')

There were also those who wanted to lead me into saying nice things above Steve and Sheila: ('They're such a nice couple, aren't they'), and those who wanted me to slag them off by contradicting the very same phrase. (*Translation:* 'They're not really as nice as they pretend to be, are they? Tell me something that will show how rotten they really are.')

I had one moment of fun with one nasty 'artist' twit, who said in a confidential way: 'Of course, your Uncle tries hard with his carvings, but what a pity about his talent' (*translation:* 'Let's be rotten about your Uncle together'), to which I said: 'That's funny, that's exactly what he said about you.'

That put the bloke out, but after that the party got boring, so I threw up over a woman and went to bed.

150

Wednesday 25th

Chaos today.

Last night's 'do' put a few cats among a few pigeons. Apparently the artist twit I had a go at last night is Aunt Sheila's art teacher at evening class, and she think's he's so wonderful and the sun shines out of his ears. So, when she heard from him what I told him Steve had said about his paintings, she was livid. I woke up this morning to hear her yelling at Steve, saying he was jealous of Roland (this artist twit) because he had 'real talent'. This got up Uncle Steve's nose and he said if she thought Roland's paintings showed any signs of talent then she either needed glasses or a brain transplant.

He then said it was a pity I'd been sick over

151

Roland's wife (so that's who the woman was) instead of over one of Roland's paintings as it would have improved it.

Decided it was time to get in on the action, so I hurried downstairs and strolled into the kitchen with a cheery 'Hello'. They both shut up, so I stirred things up by being 'apologetic', and said, 'I'm sorry I was sick last night. I tried to get to the toilet in time. I hope that woman and her husband weren't upset; they seemed a nice couple.'

This brought a strangled noise from Steve, and Sheila said, 'You'll have to excuse your Uncle Steve, he's feeling a little under the weather this morning.' (*Translation:* 'We've had a row and I'm going to rub his nose in it.')

This being too good an opportunity to miss, I threw in an 'innocent': 'Is that man a good artist? He seemed to know a lot about painting.'

That did it. Steve burst out with; 'That man wouldn't know good art if you banged him over the head with it.'

Sheila came in sharply with, 'I really don't think our nephew is interested in your views on someone else's talent.' (*Translation:* 'Shut up, Steve'), so I came in with: 'Oh, but I am.'

At this Steve opened his mouth to really lay into Roland, but Sheila went all tight-lipped and grim-faced and cut in with, 'I really think we all ought to get on. There's a lot to do in the house today.' (*Translation:* 'Steve, shut up. You and I will argue about this in private later.')

Steve shut up, but the look on his face said an awful lot.

Thursday 26th
Day off today. Steve and Sheila not talking.

Went into town on my own for the afternoon. Annoyed a bloke in a café by making a cup of coffee last an hour. He kept coming up and saying, 'Would you like anything else?' (*Translation:* 'Order something or get out'.) I smiled politely and said 'No' every time.

When I finally left and paid, he said, 'Service isn't included.' (*Translation:* 'I want a tip'), to which I smiled politely and said, 'Quite right too. Give the customer a choice,' and just walked out.

Friday 27th
Found out yesterday afternoon Sheila went to visit Roland ('to make sure his wife wasn't upset over Tuesday night').

This led to an almighty row, with Steve accusing Sheila of fancying Roland. Great stuff. Plates and saucepans flying all over the place.

Steve finally said, 'I think we ought to leave this until we've both cooled down.' (*Translation:* 'I'm losing, so let's call a truce.').

I said (helpfully), 'Is there anything I can do?', to which Steve said, 'Yes. Go and drown yourself.'

I turned to Sheila appealingly and said, 'Auntie Sheila, do you think I deserved that?' She said, 'Yes.' So, another successful project: two people made honest.

Saturday 28th
Well, all good things come to an end. Today I went home. Uncle Steve and Aunt Sheila didn't

say, 'It was wonderful having you here', so I guess they're cured.

My parents, on the other hand, said, 'It's good to have you back', which I know to be a lie, meaning 'Oh no, not you again'.

I can see I'll have to take these people in hand.

Well, there you have it. By now you should be
able to understand Grown-upese (a language on
its own). If adults still baffle you sometimes
when what they say is obviously untrue – or just
doesn't make any sense – then check again with
this book for a translation.

If their contradictory words still have you
wondering, then it could be that your particular
grown-up is more cunning, more cowardly, more
hypocritical, or simply more stupid, than most.

In which case, why not keep a log yourself of
things *your* grown-ups say, and what they really
mean:

My parents say ....

       but mean ....

My teacher says ....

       but means ....

My gran says ....

       but means ....

Politicians say ....

       but mean ....

All the best, and don't let them beat you!

3. MORE
WAYS TO HANDLE
GROWN-UPS

INTRODUCTION

Our first two books, *How To Handle Grown-Ups*, and *What Grown-Ups Say And What They Really Mean*, were mainly concerned with advice on how to handle your grown-ups in your own home, or at school.

However, we were deluged with letters from children saying that their problem was not at home – where they could always hide somewhere safe (like in their own room) – but when their grown-ups took them out somewhere.

We saw at once that there was a need for a book to advise young people on how to get their own way with grown-ups when *away* from home. The real need was to make sure that grown-ups were stopped from taking their children to places they didn't want to go (e.g. visiting boring relatives, being dragged around art galleries, or being made to be a bridesmaid or a page at a wedding).

In this book you will find plenty of ways to make sure that you will never again be invited out to any of these awful occasions. So, here it is: How Not To Get Invited Back, or *More Ways to Handle Grown-Ups: Out and About*.

The best of luck with your grown-ups!

Jim and Duncan Eldridge

How to MAKE SURE YOU ARE NOT INVITED BACK TO THE home of BORING RElatives And Friends of your PARENTS

TR UNCLE JIM

For some strange reason parents insist on taking their children to visit relatives and friends of theirs who are among the most boring people the human race has ever produced. What is worse, parents insist during these visits that their children: (a) dress in 'smart' uncomfortable clothes; (b) remain silent during the visit, with only the occasional spot of quiet breathing allowed.

It has always struck us that this is a perfect example of the hypocrisy of parents. They spend years teaching their children to walk and talk, and as soon as they can they tell them: 'Sit down and keep quiet.'

Why do they insist on their children accompanying them on these awful visits? When their child complains, parents say, 'If you don't shut up we'll leave you here and go without you.' When the child says, 'Good, that's what I want,' the parents ignore this remark and force their offspring into hideous clothes, bundle them into the nearest form of transport, and force them to endure mind-numbing boredom for what seems like two eternities.

Well this is how to get out of it. This is how to make sure that after one visit you are never invited back again.

A. Break Things

Aim for something irreplaceable, like an heirloom that has been in the family for generations. If there are none lying around, go for something expensive. But remember to apologize afterwards ('I'm so sorry, I didn't realize it was there.'). This will make it impossible for the awful relative/friend to ask you or your parents to pay for it. (On the other hand, if your parents have to pay for it, it serves the same purpose: they won't let you go back.)

Some useful targets are:

chairs
cups
saucers
plates
ornaments
floorboards
bannisters
records: however, first make sure that any record you smash is one of the grown-ups'

favourites. If you 'accidentally' break, bend, warp
or sit on a record that one of them has always
hated, but been afraid to get rid of because the
other one's mother gave it to them as a present,
then this will defeat your object. You will be
invited back, taken on tours through the house
and given all the things they hate to look at (e.g.
book-ends from Uncle Arthur).

There are plenty of things that you can
dismantle with one sharp pull. For all of them

you can use the same excuse, 'It came off in my hand.' Useful targets include:
    door handles
    door bells
    toilet cistern handles
    toilet-roll holders
    handles of cups
    the whiskers of ornamental animals.

B. Ruin Furniture

Stick the following on your hosts' furniture:
    food
    vomit
    chewing gum
    nose pickings
    drink (preferably something sticky)
    dirty soles of shoes.

Drop any of the above on to cloth-covered furniture, curtains or carpets. (*Note:* It's a waste of time dropping/sticking them on shiny wood, metal or plastic furniture. The marks can be wiped off too easily.)

Once your chosen substance hits the material (carpet, chair cover, or whatever), smear it in to make it permanent.

C. Food

Eat disgus   gly: keep your mouth open at all times, and   ake sure it is always crammed to overflowi. : so that food falls out as you eat.

Talk as you eat: spray food with every word. Talk to lots of people while eating, it sprays the food in more directions.

Choke on food: go purple in the face, clutch your throat and fall on the floor, moaning, 'I've been poisoned!'

Don't eat any of the food. This always offends someone who has spent hours preparing it.

Pull funny faces as you eat to let everyone know you think the food is horrible.

Put other people off their food by talking about disgusting subjects at meal-times (e.g. nose pickings, diseases involving open wounds, what goes into a sausage).

Peer at the food carefully, then pick something out, examine it, and say, 'There's a mouse dropping in this.' Then eat it.

Put lots of *tomato ketchup* on everything.

Say things like:

'The food's not as bad as Mum/Dad said it would be.'

'Mum/Dad said you wouldn't give us much to eat.'

'Luckily we ate before we came.'

'I suppose lots of people like this kind of thing.'

'Did you know this sort of food is bad for you?'

'I'm sure I saw something move on my plate.'

D. Criticize the House

Direct

'Don't you ever clean the house?'

'What's that terrible smell? Doesn't your toilet work?'

'Your windows need washing. Do you leave them until it rains?'

'These chairs look a bit cheap.'

'What awful wallpaper.'

'Is this house due to be demolished?'

'This table's got woodworm.'

'Look, that's a rat dropping. I recognize it because we're studying rats in biology.'

'Aren't your floors filthy.'

'Do we have to drink out of these cups?'

Subtle

'Weren't these the chairs that were reported stolen on *Police 5*?'

'I don't think this house is as big a mess as Mum and Dad said it was.'

'I know the name of a window cleaner if you want one.'

'I'm sure this house will look very nice when it's finished.'

'I shouldn't worry what other people say about your house, so long as you like it, that's all that matters.'

'Was this furniture here when you moved in, or did the dustmen deliver it by mistake?'

'Are you against using cleaning materials for environmental reasons?'

'I suppose after a while you build up an immunity to germs and dirt.'

'I expect it must be lots of fun to get your furniture from jumble sales.'

'Isn't it amazing how quickly a house gets dirty?'

'Has your vacuum cleaner broken?'

'I don't care what other people say, *I* think your house looks . . . all right.'

E. Indulge in Embarrassing Topics of Conversation

'My grandfather suffers from piles. He has to sit on a rubber cushion with a hole in it.'

'Our cat's got diarrhoea.'

'I hear your aunt's in prison.'

'I thought we might have to eat out of a trough because Mum says you eat like pigs here.'

'They found head lice at our school last week, and now I feel all itchy.'

'I hear you're very poor.'

'Is that really a wig?'

'How does a fish drink? I only ask because Dad says you drink like one and I've never seen it before.'

'I hear that you voted for (*their favourite political party*). My Dad says he always wondered what sort of people voted for them.'

'Our dog's got fleas.'

'My Dad says unions should be banned by law from going on strike.'

'Did you cut your hair like that on purpose or did it get caught in something?'

'You're not getting a divorce after all, then?'

'My Grandad was arrested again last week.'

'What did you have electric shock treatment for?'

'This boy in our class has got this rare illness that means wax keeps oozing out of his nose.'

'I see your hair transplant wasn't very successful.'

'Was your daughter very heart-broken when her fiancé dumped her?'

'I think we ought to ban all nuclear weapons.' (*or*) 'I think nuclear weapons are a good thing.' (*This depends on the views of your hosts. Pick the one they will totally disagree with.*)

'Mum says that (*your hosts' favourite singer or group*) are rubbish.'

'Dad says that he can't understand what sort of idiot watches (*your hosts' favourite TV programme*).'

How To Avoid FURTHER VISITS To MUSEUMS AND ART GALLER~~YS~~IES

Grown-ups take children to museums and art galleries for two reasons:

1. *To impress the other people* in the museum or gallery with their knowledge as they spout out facts aloud to you. (e.g. 'That picture was painted by Picasso. You can tell by the sort of shapes he paints.' They forget to add that an even bigger clue to the identity of the artist is the signature in the corner.)
2. *To try to educate you.* Your argument that a comic has as much educational value as a visit to the museum is usually disregarded by adults, who all pretend that they never ever read comics when they were children but only Good Books by people like Shakespeare.

To get out of being dragged on further visits to museums or art galleries, it is worth concentrating on the above points, by:

1. Embarrassing your grown-up in front of other people.
2. Making it appear that your education has been terrible, and it's all your grown-up's fault.

The ultimate aim, of course, is to get yourself banned from these places after your first visit, then you won't be allowed back in anyway.

A. Museums

Embarrassing Things to Say in Museums

'Why have they only got old stuff here! Can't they afford new things?'

'If the Ancient Chinese were so clever why didn't they invent a fork?'

'That doesn't look like a Stone Age axe head; it looks like a lump of rock out of our garden.'

Go up to an ancient statue of a nude woman (usually a goddess) and say, 'Her boobs aren't as big as my teacher's.'

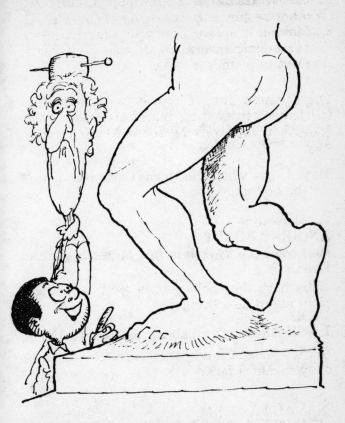

*Awful Jokes to Crack in Specialist Museums, or
Museum Departments*

PREHISTORY
Do you know what came after the Iron Age and
the Bronze Age!
The Saus-age.

ANCIENT GREECE

(When your grown-up is looking at Greek vases and urns.)

What's a Grecian urn?
About fifty pounds a week.

ENGLISH HISTORY

Do you know which King was a nut?
William the Conker.

Do you know where the Magna Carta was signed?
At the bottom.

ANCIENT EGYPT

How come the Egyptians had Mummies but no Daddies?

INDIA

I see this section's all about the Hindu religion. What's a Hindu?
It lays eggs.

NAVAL MUSEUM

What do you get if you cross the Atlantic with the Titanic?
Halfway.

MILITARY MUSEUM

We had our electricity bill in last week. My Dad called it The Charge of the Light Brigade.

Things to Say in Each Museum Department that are Wrong and will Embarrass the Grown-up with you

PREHISTORY
'Did you know that you and I are descended from apes? Especially you.'

VIKING
'Did you know that the Vikings' boats were made of raspberry jelly so they would have something to eat if they got hungry?

ANCIENT ROME
'Did you know that an Ancient Roman invented the first ever motor car, but because no one invented petrol for another two thousand years he thought it would never work, so he dropped the idea? His name was Julius Caesar Mercedes.'

'Did you know that Roman roads were built straight because they hadn't invented the curved kerbstone to go around corners?'

ANCIENT GREECE
'Did you know that the ancient Greeks had one glass eye each?'

ANCIENT EGYPT
'Did you know that the Egyptian Empire was named after the Empire cinema in London?'

ANCIENT BRITAIN
'Did you know that Stonehenge is made of Plasticine?'

SAXON
'Did you know that the Saxons invented the saxophone?'

ENGLISH HISTORY
'Did you know that the Black Death was caused by a load of mouldy pork sausages?'

'Did you know that Henry VIII had nine wives and they were all called Jane, except for eight of them?'

'Did you know that Sir Walter Raleigh invented the bicycle?'

ANCIENT BIBLICAL WORLD
'Did you know that Alexander the Great's Dad was called Alexander the Greater? He was actually named after an ancient Egyptian cheese grater, but they couldn't spell properly in those days.'

'Did you know that the Hittites were so called because they used to hit everyone?'

'Did you know that all the coins made before Jesus Christ was born have BC after the date on them?'

SCIENCE
'Did you know that gravity wasn't invented until AD 700? Before that everyone used to float in the air, which is why no one wore shoes.'

'Did you know that the Angles invented geometry?'

176

AMERICA

'Did you know that Ancient Mexicans believed that if you unwound your ear your nose fell off?'

'Did you know that when Christopher Columbus discovered America he was really looking for Russia but he had his map upside down?'

FRANCE

'Did you know that Joan of Arc was Noah's wife?'

'Did you know that Louis XIV of France was known as the Sun King because he was the son of a King?

CHINA

'Did you know that the Great Wall of China was only meant to be 50 metres long, but the builders had lost the part of the plans that told them how to end it?'

'Did you know that Ghenghis Khan used to play in goal for Real Madrid?'

EXPLORERS

'Did you know that Marco Polo invented the Mars Bar 300 years ago, but it didn't become popular because no one wanted a Mars Bar with a hole in it.'

B. Art Galleries

Stand by a painting and say, 'Is this the painting they found out was a fake? Why is it still hanging here?'

Breathe on a sculpture and polish it with your sleeve.

Say in a loud voice to your grown-up, 'Are you sure we can get away with stealing this painting?'

Stick chewing gum on a sculpture.

Go up to one of the attendants (usually to be found slumped on a chair) and say, 'What's this sculpture supposed to be? It looks like a load of old clothes with a pumpkin for a head.'

Stand some distance from a famous abstract painting and say loudly, 'Is this the one you said was a load of rubbish. I see what you mean when you said it's all just a con trick. Fancy paying someone thousands of pounds just for spilling a few pots of paint.'

Look out for a modern sculpture with a hole in it, and stick your head through it. If your head gets stuck, so much the better, as they will have to call the Fire Brigade to cut the sculpture into pieces to get you out.

Find a famous portrait (e.g. the Mona Lisa) and take out a felt-tip pen as if you are about to draw a moustache on it.

Sit on a big sculpture and say, 'Gee up!'

Say, 'How much do you reckon the frame's worth? It's better than the picture.'

178

Say, 'If you look carefully you can see it was done by Paint-By-Numbers.'

Pretend to recognize people you know in paintings:

'That woman holding that swan looks just like the woman who lives next door. She doesn't wear many clothes either, does she, Dad?'

'That man having his head chopped off looks just like my teacher.'

'The dog in that picture is like the one that lives next door to the greengrocer. Remember, it did a wee up against our front door.'

'See the ant in that picture? My friend had one just like that in a matchbox.'

Make jokes about, or mispronounce, the names of famous artists as you look at the paintings:

Constable: 'Fancy a policeman painting pictures like that.'
or
If that's the best he could paint, no wonder he never got promoted to Sergeant.'

Picasso: Pronounce it 'Pickaxe-o'.

Whistler: Say the name, give a whistle, then laugh at your own joke.

Leonardo da Vinci: Pronounce it as Leonard (or Lenny) day Vinky.

Vincent van Gogh: Have lots of fun with this. Attempt to pronounce his last name as many times as possible. The record is held by a boy in Scotland who was able to mispronounce the name no less than 27 times (Goff, Goof, Guff, Gug, Gog, Golf, Go, Gowf, Gudge, etc). As a result his embarrassed father was barred from the local Art Gallery and his local Art Club.

C. Museums *and* Art Galleries

Things to Do to Embarrass your Grown-Up

Drop a load of tiny round boiled sweets on the floor. They will roll all over the place and every time someone treads on one they will crunch it underfoot. This also works well with marbles, although with marbles people tend to fall over when they tread on them.

Call out, 'Has anyone seen my pet mouse (*or snake, or rat*)? It seems to have escaped from my pocket.' This will clear the room you are in within seconds.

If there is a really large exhibition hall with a polished floor, slide across it.

Test the echo in the big rooms by shouting.

Things to Say to Embarrass your Grown-Up

'How much longer have we got to stay here?'

'Either the drains in this place don't work or someone's just made a bad smell.'

'When there was a programme about this place on the telly you turned it over to *East Enders*.'

'Aren't these places boring.'

'Don't you get some odd people in these places.'

'You said that only posers go to these places.'

'Where are the toilets in this place?'

'This place used to be a hospital for contagious diseases.'

How to Avoid BEING TAKEN BACK TO VISIT PEOPLE IN HOSPITAL

For some reason grown-ups always want to take children with them when they go hospital visiting. They do this in spite of the fact that hospital authorities hate children and either ban them from the wards, or else insist that they sit on uncomfortable chairs and keep absolutely still while everyone is gathered around the bed of the patient.

Often the person you are taken to visit in hospital is an adult that you would never want to visit even when they were fit and healthy, so why grown-ups think you would want to see them when they are ill and spotty and in plaster and generally Yuk is a complete mystery. Also, the last thing an ill adult would want is a visit from someone like you. Such a visit would quite likely cause them to have a relapse.

Because of this it is in the patient's interests (as well as yours) that you do your best to get out of visiting people when they are in hospital.

The exceptions to this are:

1. People you like.

2. Rich people who might leave you something in their will.

Sooner or later your grown-ups will insist on taking you hospital visiting. It is difficult (but not impossible: see *Before You Get to the Hospital*) to get out of this very first visit. If you cannot, remember that good dodgers should be able to use this first visit to make sure that they never again have to go hospital visiting.

A. Before You Get to the Hospital

This is an important part of the strategy. Make sure that your parents know that you don't want to go hospital visiting because:

Hospitals are full of ill people, which means they are full of germs, which means you are bound to catch something.

You have a fear of hospitals which brings you out either in spots or stripes.

It is a long way and the journey will make you feel ill. (This excuse also applies to museums, art galleries, visits to relatives, etc.)

It will upset you to see your favourite aunt/uncle/granny/neighbour lying in a hospital bed.

The doctors and nurses in that hospital are horrible to children.

Children aren't allowed to go visiting in that particular hospital.

If none of these works and your hard-hearted grown-ups insist on taking you, then make the journey as difficult as you can:

If going by train, tell them the train is on the wrong platform.

If going by car or coach, keep wanting to go to the toilet, or be sick.

For further suggestions, see the Section *How To Make Sure That Your Future Journeys With Your Parents Are Shorter and Better* (page 56).

B. At the Hospital

Things to Do

The patient will be sure to have a bowl of fruit by the bed. Eat their fruit. If they have sweets, eat their sweets as well.

Make rude noises as if you are suffering from wind.

Scrape the legs of your chair on the polished floor. It makes a terrible screeching sound that will set everyone's teeth on edge.

'Accidentally' knock things over (e.g. a vase full of flowers; the patient's dinner).

Give the patient a friendly pat on whatever part of them is in plaster (e.g. broken leg, broken arm).

Fall asleep while the patient is in the middle of talking to you. Even better, lie on their bed and fall asleep.

Things to Say

'That man/woman in the next bed looks really ill. What's he/she got?'

'Do you mind if I take a photograph of you? Just in case.'

Make rude remarks about the hospital staff in stage whispers (i.e. just loud enough for it to be heard): 'I don't like the look of that doctor. He looks like the butcher who lives down our street,' and, 'Does that nurse drink? Her eyes are all bloodshot.'

'Are you going to have tubes and things sticking out of you when we come again?'

'I know someone else who was in this same ward. He died.'

'You're better off in here than outside. Outside everyone is saying terrible things about you behind your back.'

'I didn't bring you any flowers because I didn't think you'd be well enough to appreciate them, and it seemed a pity to waste the money.'

'I bought you some sweets to cheer you up, but I ate them on the way here.'

'Do they have an undertaker attached to this hospital?'

'Are you sure you don't want me to call the nurse? You look terrible.'

'The plants in your garden have all withered and died since you've been in hospital.'

'Mum says she never knew you had a clean pair of pyjamas/nightdress.'

'This is one of the filthiest hospitals I've ever seen. Didn't the Health Minister threaten to close it down last year?'

'Is your house locked up safely? They've had a lot of burglaries in your street since you've been in here.'

'I hope your operation went well, beause I read in the newspaper that this hospital's run out of blood.'

'Did you know that the majority of patients leave hospital in a worse state of health than when they went in. It's a fact.'

'Did you know that this hospital is where they train student doctors. I hope they haven't given you one of these awful new students who does everything wrong.'

'Have they had this ward disinfected after that case of plague they had in here last week?'

'Have they told you yet what you've *really* got wrong with you?'

'I looked up your symptoms in a medical book and according to that you're seriously ill.'

'I think they're giving you the wrong treatment.'

'According to a friend of mind whose Mum's a doctor, pretty soon you'll start to lose all feeling all over. Once that sets in, you've had it.'

'I overheard someone say you ought to be sent home. They reckon you're not ill at all, it's all in your mind.'

'Dad said you ought to be ashamed. He said you're taking up a bed that could be used for someone who was really ill.'

'I looked up what you've got in a medical dictionary. It's worse than you thought.'

Tell Stories of Operations and Hospital Treatments that went Wrong

'I read about this man who went into hospital for an operation on his nose. By mistake they removed his leg.'

'This woman went in for an operation on her stomach and the surgeon left his rubber glove sewn up inside her.'

'You know why surgeons wear masks, don't you? It's so that they can't identify a surgeon who does an operation wrong.'

'There was this hospital where all the patients caught food poisoning because the kitchens were in a filthy state.'

'There was a woman who went into hospital for an appendix operation. She'd heard that they got so many operations wrong that she had written all over her body: "It's my appendix you should be operating on." Even then they got it wrong.'

'Be careful what drugs they give you; some of them have terrible side effects. There was one hospital where they tested these drugs on this man, and his head turned into a cabbage.'

How NOT To Get Invited To WEDDINGS AND Christenings

How to get out of being a Bridesmaid or a Page

Sooner or later you will be invited to be a bridesmaid or a page for someone's wedding. The word 'invited' is another example of adult hypocrisy. What it means is that you *will* do this job. If you do, it is a fate worse than death.

The trouble is, if you are successful at it once, you will be asked to do it again at the weddings of other cousins, aunts or uncles. To avoid this it is of the utmost importance that you do it all wrong the first time.

Stand on the bride's train. (This is the long part of her dress that drags along behind her.) Do it suddenly and she will fall over. Do it right from her entrance into the church and she will feel as if she is dragging a ton of coal behind her.

Trip the bridegroom up. With a bit of luck he will fall into the bride, who will crash into her father, who will fall on to the vicar, and the whole lot will tumble down like a row of falling dominoes.

Mumble and mutter under your breath, but just loud enough to irritate the bride and groom.

Hum a song tunelessly.

Pretend to find a ring on the church floor (use a curtain ring), and say, 'The best man must have dropped this ring.' It will cause havoc.

Use superstition. Whisper things to the bride like, 'There's a black cat over there in the church. Isn't it unlucky on your wedding day?' and, 'They said it was lucky if the bride was kissed by a chimney sweep, so I've arranged for a chimney sweep to call on you. Unfortunately he can't make it until just after midnight.'

How to get out of being a Guest at a Wedding or Christening

Although not in the same league as being a bridesmaid or page, being a guest at a wedding is still pretty awful. The same goes for being a guest at a christening. For one thing, both ceremonies are so boring. Who really wants to see a baby having its head washed, especially when you have to stand in a cold and draughty church for what seems like weeks?

Make sure that your first 'invitation' to such an event is your last.

Embarrassing Things to Say at Weddings

'You'd think she'd have done better for herself than him.' (*Or:* 'You'd think he'd have done better for himself than her.')

191

'Does he know about her other boyfriends?' (*Or:* 'Does she know about his other girlfriends?')

'Has she told him about her disease?' (*Or:* 'Has he told her about his disease?')

'I hope the food is better than at the last wedding reception I was at. It was so bad there that I ate the bride's bouquet.'

'If he's the best man then why isn't she marrying him?'

'Kiss the bride? With that face? I'd rather kiss the vicar.'

'I'm not surprised the bride's father is giving her away. He'd be lucky to find anyone who'd pay for her.'

'She always said she liked the simple things in life. Dad says now she's marrying one.'

'Mum says that the bridegroom's been left at the altar so many times he can find his way down the aisle blindfolded.'

'The bridegroom has forgotten to take the price sticker off the bottom of his shoe.'

'Look at the bride's father. His trousers are undone.'

'I wouldn't have thought the bride would have worn that colour dress, it shows up all her spots.'

'Have you ever noticed how brides always choose bridesmaids uglier than them so that they will look pretty. She must have had a tough time finding those bridesmaids.'

Awful Jokes to Crack at Weddings

(*Note:* the joke is to be said loudly, with a terrible cackling laugh at the end of it.)

Where do rabbits go when they get married? On a bunnymoon.

What do you call spiders when they get married? Newlywebs.

Did you hear about the two octopuses who got married. They walked down the aisle hand in hand, hand in hand, hand in hand, hand in hand, hand in hand, hand in hand, hand in hand, hand in hand.

Do you know how many wives a man gets when he gets married?
16. 4 better, 4 worse, 4 richer, 4 poorer.

Embarrassing Things to Say at Christenings

'What an ugly baby. Who do you reckon he takes after?'

'Why is the vicar putting water on it? Didn't they wash it before they brought it here?'

193

'Are you sure it's a baby? I'm sure I've seen similar things in the zoo.'

'Either that baby's uglier than I thought, or the vicar's holding it the wrong way up.'

'If that man's the baby's godfather, does that mean he's in the Mafia?'

'I bet the vicar drops the baby in the font.'

'I think the baby's just filled its nappy.'

'Why have we come here? You said you didn't believe in christenings.'

Awful Jokes to Crack at Christenings

(*Note:* as with the awful jokes at weddings, tell them in a loud voice, and add a terrible cackling laugh at the end.)

My friend was christened Glug Glug. The vicar fell in the font.

Do you know how a baby plays football?
By dribbling.

When the Czar of Russia and his wife, the Czarina, had twins, do you know what they were called?
Czardines.

Do you know where baby apes sleep?
In apricots.

Why is a baby like our old car?
Because they've both got a rattle.

Dad said their baby was born at home, but after his Mum saw it she had to be taken to hospital.

Embarrassing Things that can be Said either at Weddings or Christenings

'Can't they afford heating in this place?'

'Why is that priest wearing a dress?'

'Look at those numbers in that frame on the wall.' (*Note:* these are the numbers of the hymns.) 'They're just like the numbers of the winning horses when you take me to the betting shop.'

'These seats are so hard my bottom's getting sore.'

'How long have we got to keep kneeling? My leg's going stiff.'

'When do we eat?'

'Is this the place where you said you once practised Black Magic?'

'Do they have a collection? Is that how the vicar gets his wages?'

'Dad, have you told Mum how you got thrown out of the church choir when you were my age?'

Embarrassing Things to Do at Weddings or Christenings

Talk all the time. When people say 'Shh' to you, look around to see who they are shushing.

Sing very loudly and out of tune when everyone sings the hymns. Even better, sing a different hymn from everyone else.

Start to scratch. This will irritate the people around you. Say to them apologetically: 'I'm sorry, but I've got fleas.' They will then start to scratch as well.

Yawn. This is very catching. Soon everyone in the church will be yawning. With a bit of luck they will all fall asleep.

How Best to OFFEND PEOPLE with YOUR CLOTHING

This is very important. Badly dressed children are not welcome in other people's houses. So, the worse dressed you are, the less welcome you will be.

Here are a few examples of just how badly you can dress:

Messy
Just before entering anywhere you wish to be
thrown out of, roll in mud. Usually wherever
there is mud there are trees with loads of leaves
lying under them. When you are covered in mud,
roll in the leaves. When you stand up you will
resemble a bush. Now go in.

Food-stained
Spread as much food over your clothes and your face, hair and hands as you can. Give the appearance of having eaten out of a trough blindfolded, using a shovel.

Torn
Tear off a sleeve. Split the seams of your clothing. Pull out the stuffing from any padded clothes. Make it look as if you were caught up in a lawn mower.

Garish

Wear the most hideous and brightly decorated clothes that you can find. Mix combinations in the worst possible taste. Dye your hair bright colours. Paint your face. Wear loads of flashing ornaments.

Punk

Although now pretty outdated, this style is still calculated to drive most adults into a fury. Wear shredded clothes, and T-shirts and jackets with rude slogans on them. Shave half the hair off your head. Pin your clothes together with as many safety pins as you can bear the weight of without falling over.

Smelly
Similar to Messy, except instead of mud, find a dung heap to roll about in. Put a few dead fish in your pockets. Smear dog mess on the soles of your shoes.

Paper Bag over the Head
Find a large paper bag, cut out two holes for
your eyes, and put it over your head. This
always makes grown-ups worry: what is under
the paper bag?

Nude
(Although the chances of you actually getting anywhere in this outfit are very small.)

HOW TO GET OUT OF GOING

~~ANYWHERE~~ ANYWHERE

The basic rule here is to pretend to be ill. How ill you pretend to be depends on where your parents plan to take you, and how long you want to be thought of as 'ill'. Remember, if you pretend to have bubonic plague one day, do not be surprised if your parents get suspicious if you say you are all right the next morning to go to a party.

The best illnesses to fake are the following:

Measles, etc. (anything with spots)
Use a felt tip pen to put spots on your face. Make sure you use the correct colour (e.g. reddish-brown). Green spots are very suspicious and might make your grown-up think you are a visitor from another planet.

Sprained Ankle
Limp and go 'ouch' every now and then. Lean heavily on furniture and other objects as you walk along.

Sprained Arm or Shoulder
Clutch your arm to your side and wince and moan a lot. Tell everyone that you are unable to write.

Colds and Flu

Squirt water up your nose so that it keeps running down. Spread vaseline around your nostrils to make your nose look wet and shiny. If you are given a thermometer to take your temperature, put it on a radiator or a hot water bottle first.

Vomiting

Rub flour or a white cream on to your face to give you a very pale appearance. When you get into the toilet, leave the door open so that the retching noises you make can be clearly heard by your grown-ups.

Diarrhoea

We will not go into nasty details here. Just keep going into the toilet a lot, and stay there for ages and ages.

Stomach Ache

Bend over, clutch your stomach, moan, groan and writhe in agony. Complain of pains that are 'like a knife'.

Concussion

First you need to tell your grown-ups that you banged your head earlier. (*Note*: you do not actually have to have banged your head, just tell them you did.) Once they know that you have been injured in this way, wander about in a dazed manner, with a glazed look in your eyes. Mutter things like 'Where am I?' and 'Who are you?' Walk into walls.

HoW to MAKE sure that future Journeys with YOUR PARENTS ARE SHORTER AND BETTER

The aim of these dodges is to ensure that any journey you have to make with your grown-ups is as short and as pleasant as possible.

The rules here are:-

1. If the first journey is by cramped coach, make sure that the journey is so awful that in future they will travel by train (First Class, naturally, in order to keep you away from people); or by car (a large roomy comfortable car, of course).

2. If the journey is a really long one, persuade them to take a plane.

Here's how to do it:

While Waiting for the Coach or Train

Keep your grown-ups in a state of nervousness by calling out, 'That looks like our one!' every few minutes.

Keep saying, 'Are you sure this is the right stop (*or* platform)?'

Say, 'I just overheard someone say the drivers are on strike.'

Complain about the cold weather, even if it is boiling hot.

Hide any luggage. This will drive your grown-ups into a panic.

Go to the toilet, and wait until the coach or train arrives before re-appearing.

On the Coach or Train

Keep asking to use the toilet.

Keep telling your grown-up (in a loud voice) that you feel sick.

Complain that there is nowhere for you to stretch out.

Go for walks up and down the aisles 'to stretch my legs, otherwise I'll get cramp.' As you walk, tread on people's feet and trip over their luggage.

Go up to strangers and say, 'Would you like to see my pet cockroach.'

Find a passenger who wants to be left in peace to read a book, and start talking to them.

Open the windows and freeze everyone.

Sit next to someone and pretend to fall asleep. Let your head rest on their shoulder. Snore. Dribble on their clothing.

Tell the other passengers that you have an infectious disease.

Pretend to search for your missing mouse (or lizard, or some other small animal).

This one needs preparation beforehand. Get a polythene bag and put vegetable salad in mayonnaise into it. In the middle of your journey suddenly say, 'Urgh! I feel sick!' Pick up the polythene bag (carefully concealing its contents), put your head into it, and pretend to be sick. Then take out a spoon and start to eat the mayonnaise salad.

Let off stink bombs.

Blow bubbles all over the other passengers.

Keep asking for things to be handed down to you from the luggage rack, and then put back up again.

Make loud comments to your grown-ups about the other passengers. ('Hasn't that man got a big nose'; 'Look at that terrible dress that woman's wearing', etc.)

Ask to borrow another passenger's newspaper. Then:
(a) Tear it up, telling them you are practising to be a magician. Look sorry when your 'trick' doesn't work and the newspaper remains torn into bits.
or
(b) Blow your nose into it, telling them that you have run out of paper handkerchiefs.

Tell stories about terrible coach or train disasters. ('There was this terrible train crash only last month. A train came off the rails and everyone was killed'; 'Did you hear about the coach that crashed on this motorway last year?

Terrible. Everyone died. It was owned by the same firm as this coach. That's a coincidence, isn't it?' etc.)

In a Car

1. Complaints about your Grown-Up's Driving

'You're driving too fast.'

'You're driving too slow.'

'You're too close to that car in front.'

'You should have turned left/right back there.'

'You shouldn't hold the steering wheel like that'

'Why not let Mum/Dad drive?'

'You're not sitting properly the way a good driver does.'

'You're in the wrong lane.'

'Shouldn't you have sounded your horn round that bend?'

'What colour was that traffic light we just went through? I'm sure it was red.'

'You went a bit close when you overtook that car just then'

'Don't you think it's unfair on us to drive so dangerously?'

2. General Off-Putting Comments

'Why is that lorry behind us flashing its lights at you?'

'Are you sure this is the right road?'

'Watch out, there's a police car ahead.'

'What's the time?' (To be asked at five-minute intervals.)

'Did you see what that sign said back there?'

'I think that wobbling noise is coming from one of our tyres.'

'Did you see that rare bird that nearly hit us?'

'You've just run over a hedgehog.'

'The man in that car that overtook us just now was waving at you and pointing. I wonder what he was trying to tell us?'

'My friend's family have got a much better car than ours.'

'Isn't that the wrong indicator you're using?'

'This car door's loose.'

'Was that a parking space back there?'

'What's that red light on the dashboard that keeps coming on?'

'I hope we don't get a puncture. I can't remember if I put the jack back in when I put all that stuff in the boot.'

'Careful how you reverse, I think there's a little post just behind you.'

'I think that sign said there's a hidden entrance for lorries just along this road.'

'I said we should have gone the other way.'

On an Aeroplane

It is advisable not to try any funny business on a plane because the pilot might get fed up with you and have you thrown out, or force you to ride on the wing.

How to get out of Going for Walks

For some odd reason grown-ups are obsessed with the practice of 'going for a walk'. This usually means one of two things:

A. The Country Ramble

This is a ten-mile hike across moorland and up and down mountains. It is the sort of activity that the SAS do as part of their training.

If it's not that kind of walk, it will be an equally long route march along narrow winding country lanes, and the only things you ever see are hedges two yards high. Now and then your grown-up will point out a tree to you. On these walks you are in constant danger of being run over by a tractor driven by a farmer on the lookout for walkers.

B. The City Stroll

This is a killer. It is usually a 'sight-seeing tour' in which your grown-up keeps stopping to point at buildings, and say things to you like, 'George Bernard Shaw lived there.' The fact that you haven't got the faintest idea who or what George Bernard Shaw is (or was) is brushed aside by your grown-up as he/she drags you along to another equally uninteresting building and tells you something equally boring about it.

The only thing you will get out of one of these so-called 'strolls' is sore feet from tramping on the hard pavements.

For the sake of your health both these sorts of 'walk' are to be avoided at all costs. Make sure that your first such trip is your last. Here's how to do it:

Annoying Things to Say on a Country Ramble

'I'm allergic to trees/grass/flowers/wheat/bird noises, etc.'

'The pollen in country air gives me hay fever.'

'I don't like to see how modern civilization is destroying the countryside.'

'I think the countryside ought to be dug up and concreted over.'

'I think the countryside is boring.'

'There's no fresh air out in the countryside, it always stinks of manure.'

'Aren't we trespassing?'

'Why is that angry farmer shouting at us?'

'I heard that someone was murdered around here and their ghost still haunts this place.'

'I thought I saw a sign back there saying,
"Beware of the Bull". It must be hiding behind
that big hedge.'

'That looks like quicksand up ahead.'

'You've just trod in the most enormous cowpat.'

'I think a bird's dropped something on your hair.'

Annoying Things to Say on a City Stroll

'Can't we afford to catch a bus?'

'Is there an amusement arcade around here?'

'Are we lost? We seem to be walking around these streets in circles.'

'Mind that lamp-post.'

'There's a policeman following us. I reckon he thinks we're up to something with all this walking around looking at buildings. I bet he thinks we're planning a robbery.'

'This city is full of muggers and robbers just waiting to jump out and attack us.'

'I read in the paper that there's going to be a demonstration march through these streets. The police say they're expecting violence. I think we ought to go home before the trouble starts.'

'Have you seen the huge amounts of dog mess all over the place?'

'Do you know that this area holds the record for the most people run over by cars and buses. I don't think we ought to cross any roads.'

'Please buy me that toy/outfit/camera, etc in that shop window over there.'

Annoying Things to Say that can be used on Both Country and City Walks

'I'm tired.'

'My leg hurts.'

'I've got a blister on my foot.'

'These shoes are too tight for me to walk properly.'

'These shoes are too loose and I keep falling over.'

'My shoelace has come undone again.'

'How much further have we got to walk? This is really boring.'

'Were your parents cruel to you, dragging you around like this?'

'I've got a cold coming on. I should be at home in the warm. This trudging around in this cold air will turn it into pneumonia.'

'It's going to rain.'

'I'm hungry.'

'You'll have to go on without me, I can't make it. But don't worry, I'll be all right.'

'I heard on the news that this is an earthquake zone, and they said that there's due to be an earthquake here today.'

'I'm sure I saw something fall out of your pocket back there.'

'Mum/Dad says you shouldn't be going for long walks in your bad condition of health.'

Persistently ask, 'How far is it?' every few minutes.

THE DIARY ~~or~~ OF X

PRESENTS

MoRe WAYS To HandLe GROWN UPS

Yes, folks, it's me, 'X' again. After the extracts from my diaries in *How to Handle Grown-Ups* and *What Grown-Ups Say and What They Really Mean*, in which I showed how successful I was at handling grown-ups, I thought you might like to hear about the time I had real problems with another dodger, my cousin Tracy.

Tracy is a rat and a louse and a snake and every other form of animal life I can think of. She is rotten to the core. She is also only ten years old, which should make the Universe shudder at what she will be like when she gets older.

In my opinion she is a real danger, not only to grown-ups, but to the whole human race (and any other species that happen to be about at the time). Anyway, you'll soon see for yourselves when you read these further adventures from:-

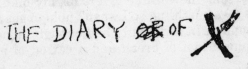

THE DIARY ~~or~~ OF X

223

Saturday 26th July

Today the school holidays start, and what a piece of really dud news I've been given to start them with: this year we are not going away anywhere because we can't afford it.

'Why can't we afford it?' I asked, and back came all these excuses: inflation, the bank rate, Dad's working hours have been cut, etc, etc. In my opinion this is all a load of old rubbish. The truth is they don't want the hassle of going away. Everyone else I know is going away: Africa, Ibiza, America, France, Cornwall, Scotland. Where am I going? Nowhere! Well I think it's rotten. After the hard year I've had at school, working my skin off to get out of everything (lessons, team games, homework) I deserve a holiday.

The only good thing about it is that my Dad and Mum will feel guilty about not taking me away, so I'll be able to play on this guilt and get them to buy me things to make up for it. Maybe if I keep asking for really expensive things they'll have second thoughts and decide it's cheaper for us all to go away on holiday.

Monday 28th July

Today Mum gave me a shopping list and a ten pound note and said that I could buy myself a present with the change. (See, I knew they'd feel guilty.)

What I did was: I bought myself the present first: some new brake levers for my bike. They cost £9 something, so I wasn't able to get all the shopping. In fact I only had enough money left to buy a loaf of bread and a carton of milk.

Mum was furious and said that I should have got the shopping *first*. Anyway, two problems solved in one go: (1) I don't think I'll be sent shopping for a while; and (2) I got the new brake levers I wanted.

Tuesday 29th July
Terrible News!

As if it wasn't bad enough that we're not going anywhere for a holiday, today Mum dropped a real bombshell on me: 'Because we felt guilty about not taking you away we've invited your cousin Tracy to stay with us for ten days. We felt you could do with some company of your own age to cheer you up.'

225

Well, I was aghast. Cheer me up?! For one thing she is not my own age, she is three years younger than me. For another thing she is horrible, a blot upon the whole human race. To land her on me for ten days is on a par with giving me boils.

'Tracy is horrible,' I pointed out. 'She is rotten.'

'But she likes being with you,' said Mum.

'Only because she hopes I'm going to catch some disease off her,' I said. 'She gave me measles once, remember?'

'She didn't do it on purpose,' said Mum.

'I bet she did,' I countered. 'It's the sort of thing she would do. What about the last time I saw her, when we went to visit her family last Christmas. She was sick all over me.'

'That was an accident.'

'Oh no it wasn't. She aimed it at me.'

Unfortunately, no matter how hard I tried, Mum didn't believe me. Just because Tracy wears pink dresses with frills and has got the sort of face that baby angels wear on the tops of Christmas trees, Mum is convinced she is Miss Wonderful. I know better.

Actually I'm not completely convinced that Mum didn't invite Tracy here as an act of revenge over the case of the shopping and the brake levers.

I will just have to be on my guard while she's here. Any suggestions of sickness or disease on her part and I shall move in with the people next door.

Wednesday 30th July

Tracy arrived today. It's seven months since I

226

last saw her (the famous Christmas vomit incident), and she hasn't improved. She still looks like a ten-year-old-angel in frilly frocks with golden hair, but this is only to fool grown-ups. Underneath she is rotten. That Christmas (the vomit one) she had treble helpings of everything by stealing food from other people's plates, and then she blamed me for it. The child is not to be trusted.

Her arrival was sickening, with her parents giving her kisses and cuddles of goodbye, and my parents giving her kisses and cuddles of hello. I hoped that with all this cuddling she'd be squashed flat and have to be taken back home, but no such luck.

Anyway, as soon as she was in, I was off. I feel safer away from wherever this blot is, and I intend to stay safe while she is here.

Thursday 31st July
Nothing much happened today. With this human fairy doll drifting around our house, I spent most of the day out on my bike.

I worked one good dodge. I put an old and bent back wheel on my bike, and then went down to the big car park. I waited until I saw someone whose rear window was all misted up start to reverse, and I stuck my bike with the bent wheel near one of his back wheels. Just as the car started to reverse, I yelled in 'pain', banged his car, and lay down on the ground.

The car screeched to a sudden stop and the bloke got out, a really worried look on his face. He looked even more worried when he saw the bent back wheel of the bike. I didn't even need to say anything, he immediately opened his wallet and thrust four five pound notes into my hand. When I looked doubtful, he hastily added another fiver to them. He kept apologizing to me while he got back in his car and drove off.

I worked the same con in another car park a bit later on, but I only got fifteen quid that time. Still, not bad for a day's work. I decided that twice was enough because more would have been greedy, and greed is the downfall of too many dodgers.

After that I went home and had tea, and kept clear of Tracy.

I also got out of doing the washing-up after tea by saying, 'I'd love to do it, Mum, but I've got an infection under my fingernail and the washing-up liquid will only make it worse. I'm also afraid that the germs from it will breed in the hot water and infect all the plates and cups and things as I wash them up.'

All in all, a pretty successful day.

Friday 1st August

Mum tried to get me to help prepare the dinner today. I 'accidently' let the water the vegetables were cooking in boil away, and they burnt and stuck to the saucepan like lumps of charcoal. The saucepan also got burnt and had to be thrown away. There was therefore no cooked dinner for Dad, Mum, Tracy and me. Luckily I had stashed away some food in my room, so I was all right. The others had to make do with sandwiches.

I think that will put an end to my being forced to do any cooking.

As a punishment for burning the dinner, I was made to vacuum clean the house, but I soon sorted that one out. I switched the cleaner to 'blow' instead of 'suck', and it chucked great clouds of grey dust all over the living room.

Another one to me.

Later:

After having written the above diary entry I was in my room, quietly minding my own business and reading my BMX magazine, when my door opened and Tracy appeared. Luckily I had hidden all traces of my secret food store. However, it wasn't food she was after.

'You're pretty good,' she said.

I was immediately suspicious.

'What at?' I asked.

'The way you get your parents to do whatever you want.'

I gave a little smirk (after all, every genius likes their talent to be recognized), and then I wiped it off my face. What was she up to?

'I don't know what you mean,' I said.

'Yes you do,' she said. 'But I'm better.'

I let this sink in.

'Better?' I asked. 'Better at what?'

'At dodging. I can get away with more than you can.'

'Sez you,' I scoffed.

'I bet I can.'

'I bet you can't.'

'How much do you bet?'

This made me stop and think a bit. Was Tracy trying to con me? Then I thought: what am I scared of? In fact there isn't much Tracy can do to con me if I take on this bet. For one thing, I am the best dodger out and it is unthinkable that Tracy could beat me. For another thing, I could always dodge on the bet and not pay up if she tries to cheat me.

I was also on my home ground, so I had a definite advantage. Without doubt, I thought, this girl must have at least a couple of screws loose even to think of challenging me on my home territory where I know everyone's weak points (essential to the art of handling grown-ups).

'All right,' I said. 'It's a bet.'

'There's one problem,' she said. 'How are we going to score points?'

I thought about it for a bit, then I said, 'Let's score on them trying to get us to go out to rotten places.'

'Why?' asked Tracy.

'Because as you're visiting they're bound to want to take us on long boring walks to show you the sights, and to visit all your relatives who live around here.'

'But that isn't fair,' she said. 'That sort of thing will only be aimed at me.'

(Curses, I thought, this girl is smarter than I thought. That had been the whole purpose of my suggesting it.)

'I'll tell you what,' she said; 'it only counts if both of us have been included in whatever visits they've got planned.'

That seemed all right with me (although not as favourable to me as my original suggestion).

'OK,' I said. 'Now, what are we betting?'

'My favourite toy against yours.'

'No fear,' I said. 'I'm not falling for that one. You pick out some terrible knitting kit that you've never used and tell me it's your favourite. I've used that one myself. No, there's only one thing worth betting: money.'

'But I haven't got any,' she said.

'You must have. Didn't your parents give you any spending money?'

'Only a few pounds.'

Which suggested to me that she was loaded, but intending to hang on to it all the time she was with us.

'All right,' I said. 'Five pounds each.'

I saw the cash register in her head click, and then she said: 'OK. Five pounds. But how do I know I can trust you to pay up if you lose?'

I must admit that more or less the same thought had occurred to me – how I was to get the money out of Tracy when she lost.

'Tell you what,' I said. 'We'll each put five pounds into an envelope, and give the envelope to someone to hold.'

'Your parents?' she suggested.

'No,' I said.

Frankly I wouldn't trust Dad and Mum with my money. It they were as broke as they said, they'd go out and spend it.

'The man in the corner shop,' I said. 'Old Mr Carstairs.'

'Can we trust him?'

'As much as we can trust anyone.'

I nearly added, more than I can trust you. Tracy was obviously not going to be very easy to con.

'All right,' she said. 'But we've got to tell him that he only gives the envelope back to the one who's got a note signed by both of us saying to hand it over.'

'But say I win and you don't sign the note?' I pointed out.

'Then I won't get my five pounds back either,' she said. Which was a good point. So we both produced our five pound notes and put them in an envelope.

'One more rule,' she said.

'What?' I said.

'Only boring places count. If we get taken to somewhere good like a film we both want to see, that's all right.'

232

'Agreed,' I said.

So the contest is on. This is going to be an easy five pounds for me. I think I can say that I am quietly confident.

Saturday 2nd August
First round today.

The first thing we did was give the envelope to Mr Carstairs at the corner shop. Then the contest started in earnest.

This morning Dad and Mum announced that they'd arranged for us all to visit the local museum today. This visit would have been one of the great non-events of the century. Our local museum has to be seen to be believed: it has two bits of broken pottery, which are claimed to be Roman remains, although they look suspiciously like one of our old flowerpots; an alleged Stone Age axe head which looks like any old lump of rock; and a signed photograph of Mahatma Gandhi, who came to our town once. I expect he got off the train at the wrong station – that's the only reason I can think of for anyone famous ever coming here. In short, our local museum gives a new meaning to the word 'boring'. So I set to work. Into the toilet, lots of retching sounds, lots of time spent shut in the toilet, and loads of staggering around clutching my stomach, a victim of sickness and diarrhoea.

'I daren't go with you,' I said. 'I daren't go too far from a toilet.'

Mum and Dad were suspicious, but I felt they were also a bit relieved not to have to endure dragging me around the museum and making caustic remarks, so they nodded and said, 'Right.

You'd better stay here. But you won't mind if we take Tracy?'

'Not at all,' I said. 'I think she'd be fascinated by it.'

At this Tracy put on a sorrowful face and said, 'Oh no, I couldn't possibly go. Not when he's so ill. I know it sounds funny, Uncle and Aunt, but would you mind if we waited until he's feeling better? If we went today I wouldn't enjoy it at all, I'd just worry all the time about him being ill and all alone here.'

'He can manage,' said Mum (a bit too unsympathetically, I thought, I suspected that what she really meant was she'd be delighted to leave me behind).

'Of course I can,' I said. 'You go off and enjoy yourself, Tracy. You'll love the museum.'

'I won't,' Tracy sighed. 'I'm very sorry. My mother says I worry too much about other people, but that's just the way I am. I would be really miserable all the time we were there, and I wouldn't be able to concentrate on anything. Not when he's so ill.'

'We understand,' said Dad. 'That's one of the drawbacks of being a caring person. We'll all go together when he's feeling better.'

So, one point each, and although Tracy did well I still feel that I have the upper hand in this contest. After all, as I said before, this is my home ground and I haven't started to play my best game yet.

Sunday 3rd August
Curses! Today I was caught out.

You remember how I said that I had an

advantage because I was on my home ground, while Tracy was playing away from home? Well this is not the case! The cunning little flea-eared, locust-faced rat has turned the situation to her advantage by playing the part of the Visitor. This means that my parents can't order her about, while I am bullied and ordered about by them as if child slavery was still the order of the day.

To show you what I mean: this morning Mum and Dad came into the living room where I was watching television and Tracy was pretending to read a book, and announced, 'We've arranged for us all to visit your Aunt Maud today, Tracy. I know she'd love to see you while you're with us.'

Good, I thought. This is where I move into a 2–1 lead because I can get out of this easily. Aunt Maud has hated the sight of me ever since I played a joke on her over her budgie. Aunt Maud has this prize budgie she is very fond of, and its cage is in a place of honour in her kitchen, something I have personally always thought was very unhygienic. On this particular occasion, when Dad and Mum had taken me to visit, Aunt Maud had said to me, 'Would you like to feed little Herbert?' which was what she calls her budgie.

'Certainly, Auntie,' I said, and trotted off to the kitchen, where I rattled the cage and made a few budgie-like chirrups and a few miaows. Then I went back into the living room, where they all gave me a puzzled look that showed all those funny noises had worried them.

'Did you feed little Herbert?' Aunt Maud asked.

'Yes, Auntie,' I said. 'I fed him to the cat.'

I thought it was funny (it was supposed to be, anyway), but Aunt Maud thought I meant it and crashed to the floor in a dead faint. It took half an hour for Dad and Mum to revive her, by which time, naturally, I was well away to somewhere safe.

Anyway, since that day Aunt Maud has not been my greatest fan. Tracy, on the other hand, couldn't possibly get out of this visit easily.

I was just smirking to myself, when Tracy said: 'Oh I'd love to visit Aunt Maud, but I really don't think I ought to go.'

'Why ever not?' said Mum. 'Aunt Maud would love to see you.'

'And I would love to see Aunt Maud,' said Tracy, 'but it would be best if I didn't go to her house.'

'Why? What's wrong with her house?' I demanded, determined that Tracy wasn't going to get out of this visit easily.

'Nothing,' said Tracy, 'except little Herbert, her beautiful little budgerigar. If I go there I may kill it.'

Well, I could understand that. The way Aunt Maud dotes on it is sickening. It is spoiled something rotten, and I have often been tempted to give it a punch in the beak just to bring it down a peg or two, but I thought Tracy was being a bit rash admitting it out loud.

'Kill it?' said Dad.

'Yes,' said Tracy. 'You see, our doctor discovered that I'm a carrier of a budgerigar disease known as wing croup, which can be fatal to the dear little birds.'

At the sight of Mum's face, obviously wondering whether she ought to disinfect everywhere in the house, Tracy added quickly, 'It doesn't affect humans at all. Or any other animals. Only budgies. It's very rare, but I'd hate to pass it on to little Herbert and be the cause of his death. I could never forgive myself. And it would upset poor Aunt Maud.'

It could also upset my chances of winning our bet. Aloud I said: 'I've never heard of wing croup. Why don't we phone Aunt Maud and see what she says?'

'I don't think that would be right,' said Tracy. 'It wouldn't be fair to alarm her. Far better to tell her I've got a cold, but that I'll see her in a few days when I'm better. Then maybe she could come here.'

'Yes, I can see that,' said Dad, nodding. 'It's a pity, though, Aunt Maud's expecting us and she'll have prepared a special tea.'

'There's no reason you three can't go,' said Tracy sweetly. 'I'll be perfectly all right on my own. You won't be long, and this really is an interesting book I'm reading.'

'Well, if you're sure you don't mind,' said Dad.

'I mind!' I pointed out.

'Tough,' said Mum. 'I'm not letting Aunt Maud down by not turning up at all.'

'Then you go and I'll stay here and look after Tracy,' I said.

'I wouldn't trust you to look after King Kong,' said Mum. 'You're going whether you like it or not. Get your anorak on.'

And that was that. No further discussion, no voting, just me forced into my anorak and whisked out of the front door. I am living in a dictatorship!

Mind, I had my own back when we got there. I put a few drops of Aunt Maud's gin in little Herbert's water and he fell off his perch, paralytic drunk, flat on his back on the floor of his cage with his feet in the air.

Once more Maud had a fainting fit, and hopefully I'm banned from going there for a good few months.

Still, the score stands at 2–1 to Tracy!

I just can't believe it. This horrible little worm is going to be a tougher opponent than I thought.

Monday 4th August

Tracy is a liar and a cheat and everything rotten! Today she moved into a two point lead, and she did it by A Lie!

Mum said that she was going to give us a treat and take us to the pictures. Now we had already agreed that this counted as being OK. Mum said she wasn't telling us what she was going to take us to see because she wanted it to be a surprise for us when we arrived at the cinema. Our local cinema has five screens and I had checked in the local paper and found out that the five films on were: a horror film, a war film, a cartoon, a car chase comedy, and some boring film about ballet.

Tracy whispered to me that she'd overheard Mum tell Dad that she was taking us to see the car chase comedy. I said, 'Good, anything so long as it's not that boring ballet film.' And, of course, that's the film that Mum took us to see! And Tracy knew all along and had lied: (a) to get me into the cinema before I knew what film we were going to see; and (b) to get me to admit that I wouldn't want to see her rotten ballet film, so that she would get the point.

So it's 3–1 to Tracy, and my reputation as the world's greatest dodger is in real danger.

I shall have to do something drastic. I only have four days left to save the situation!

Tuesday 5th August

Today I clawed back a point. The score is now 3–2 to Tracy but I'm closing fast.

I was so angry at the way that Tracy had conned me over this ballet film yesterday that I decided it would be poetic justice to use the same method against her (but altered obviously, otherwise she'd be suspicious).

I told Mum that Tracy and I had been talking, and she had told me that her dearest wish while she was staying with us was to do some brass rubbings at the local church.

What Tracy had actually said to me was: 'A month ago my Mother took me on the most boring day out I've ever been on. We did brass rubbings. You put a big sheet of paper on a grave and you have to rub it with a crayon. I got it all over my dress and it never came off. I hated it. If anyone ever shows me a brass rubbing again I shall vomit all over it.' (See, I knew she could be sick at will and that last Christmas's vomiting incident hadn't been an accident.)

Anyway, so that Tracy wouldn't be able to get out of it, I told Mum not to tell Tracy where she was taking her. 'Tell her you're taking her to buy another frilly dress. Then she'll get such a wonderful surprise when she finds herself doing a brass rubbing.'

And that was how I used Tracy's own method against her. Fortunately Mum didn't want me coming with her and Tracy, mainly because I've not been very popular at our local church since I offered to help at a service and I charged people 25p each to hire a hymn book. As a result of that I was condemned from the pulpit by the vicar and my parents claimed that they could 'never hold up our heads in public again'.

The end result of today: Tracy came back with crayon and other stains all over her dress. According to Mum, 'poor Tracy' had been taken

ill as soon as the brass rubbing started, and she had thrown up over it.

'Oh dear, oh dear,' I said. 'What a pity. Poor Tracy.'

Tracy looked at me, and if looks could have killed I'd have been dead on the spot.

I shall have to watch my step tomorrow and the next few days. Tracy is going to be after me with a vengeance.

Wednesday 6th August
Three–all!

As I expected, Tracy tried to get her own back on me today, but it backfired on her.

She was so annoyed over the brass rubbings yesterday that she told my Dad and Mum that I had been showing an interest in ancient buildings, and asked if we could both go to a talk that some idiot was giving on old buildings in our town this evening. How my parents even fell for this garbage is beyond belief. Surely they have known me long enough to know that I would never even be seen dead at such a talk! But they did fall for it, and this evening we were told to get ready for a 'wonderful' evening sitting in a draughty room at the back of the Town Hall, while this local idiot showed us slides of these really boring, uninteresting buildings.

However, I expected that Tracy would have something up her sleeve, so I was prepared.

'Wonderful!' I said with lots of enthusiasm. 'This is the talk that Tracy was telling me about earlier. We've both been really looking forward to it. I'm so glad we're going, aren't you, Tracy?'

This put her on the spot and forced her (through gritted teeth) to say that she was delighted to be going.

'But first I've just got to pop round to my friend John and lend him a history book,' I said. 'He needs it for his homework.'

Immediately Tracy saw through my plan.

'That's all right,' she said. 'We don't mind waiting until you come back from your friend's. Then we can all go together.'

'No no,' I said. 'You all go on first. That way we can make sure we get good seats in the front row. Save a chair for me and I'll be with you before it starts.'

Too late Tracy saw that her 'enthusiasm' for

this boring talk had sunk her. She had to grin and put up with it as she was being marched off to the Town Hall by Mum and Dad.

Needless to say, I never turned up. When they came back I gave them an excuse in three parts:

1. I couldn't find my history book at first.
2. John wasn't sure which part of the history book we had to work from, so I spent valuable time showing him (because I am such a wonderful bloke).
3. Because of my above unselfish act, I was late arriving at the Town Hall, and the attendant wouldn't let me in because the talk had already started. This had bitterly disappointed me.

It also bitterly disappointed Tracy. We were now on level points. One more point, and the genius to hang on to that lead, and victory (and the money) will be mine!

Thursday 7th August
Another visit to an ancient and boring relative lined up for us today, and all because of Tracy. What I cannot understand is why I have to be involved? If these idiotic relatives insist on having the human frog inflicted on them for tea, why do I have to be dragged along? Why must I suffer as well?

The relative today was my (and Tracy's) Grandad (on my Dad's side), who is enough to drive anyone mad.

He was an Air Raid Warden in the tiny village of Little Something-or-Other somewhere in East

Anglia during the Second World War. From what I can gather from other people all he ever did was wear a tin hat and walk around at night shining a torch into dark corners and telling people to turn their lights out. The fact that he was the one lighting everything up with his torch never seemed to occur to him. Also, in the whole course of the war only one bomb fell on this village, and that was dropped accidentally by a British plane. Luckily it never went off, it just fell on the local pub and demolished the roof.

So, as I say, Grandad didn't exactly have a huge part to play in the War. Unless you hear him talk about it, that is. The way that Grandad tells it, he won the whole war single-handed. According to him the Prime Minister used to phone him up and ask him how things were going, and he was always keeping battalions of fully-armed Gestapo at bay with just a shotgun and a catapult.

Anyway, Tracy and I realized there was very little either of us could do to get out of being dragged along to Grandad's. (An invitation to Grandad's house is like a Royal Command, you can only get out of it if you're dead. And even then they'd have to take your coffin along so he could check you weren't making excuses.) So we resigned ourselves to being taken, but resolved to make sure that we were never invited back again.

We agreed that we both had to do our best to make sure that we weren't invited back if we were to get a point each. I thought this was a good idea, because I couldn't imagine Tracy being badly behaved in Grandad's house, so I felt sure of winning the point and establishing a one-point lead. However, I hadn't reckoned on just how determined not to lose she was.

I have to admit, she did upset him (and my Mum and Dad) in a very subtle way by sweetly and angelically asking him embarrassing questions about his war service. It went a bit like this:

Tracy: 'Grandpa!'
Grandpa: 'Yes, Tracy?'

Tracy: 'How many Germans did you capture in the War?'

Grandpa: (*Modestly*) 'On my own, about a dozen. Although with my unit (*The Battalion of Air Raid Wardens*?) we must have captured between fifty and a hundred.'

Tracy: 'That's odd.'

Grandpa: 'What is?'

Tracy: 'Well my teacher at school was brought up in the same village, and he told us in history that no German was ever there in either of the two World Wars.' (*Here she gave an angelic simper.*) 'If you tell me when it all happened I'll be able to tell him he's wrong.'

At this there was one of those wonderful embarrassed silences as everyone coughed and tried to pretend that something else was happening. Grandad tried to cover it by claiming that it must have been another Little Something-or-Other that this teacher was talking about, but Tracy came back with: 'Oh no, it's definitely the same one, because he was a boy then and he remembers you were the Air Raid Warden. Don't you think it's funny that he can't remember the German prisoners you captured? Shall I bring him round to see you?'

She also, with the same sweet smile, suggested that he had spent the war either drunk at the local pub, or hiding in barns. It was a brilliant performance and she deserved her point. I had never seen Grandad look so angry, or Dad and Mum look so embarrassed.

I earned my point by making remarks about his personal freshness:

Me: Cor, Grandad, is that pong coming from you? Has your water been turned off?' and similar things.

Grandad was so upset at Tracy's demolition of his War Hero status, and because I wasn't as subtle, that he simply growled, 'That boy needs a good clip round the ear.' He also refused to give me the fifty pence he usually gives me when I visit.

Still, I got my point, so the score is still a draw at four points all.

Friday 8th August
At last! Tracy's last day here, and I did it! I just pipped her at the post in the last round and got that winning point!

This evening Dad and Mum suddenly sprang on us both that as it was Tracy's last night with us they were going to take us out for an evening's entertainment. At first we both felt quite pleased. The pictures? After all, we wouldn't be going to see that rotten ballet film again. But no, Dad had been given tickets to a violin recital in the local church hall. Argh! No wonder he was given the tickets. I bet they were offering people pound notes if they'd take a bunch. If there is one thing I cannot abide it is the sound of someone scraping a violin; it sounds like a cat having teeth out. I could see from Tracy's face that she felt the same way, and an idea struck me.

After tea I grabbed her on her own and whispered: 'Well, it looks as if we're caught. It's not going to be easy getting out of this, not as they're taking us out for a special occasion for your last night here. As it's a draw already, why don't we accept it? At least then neither of us loses our money.'

'I suppose so,' she sighed. 'Still, it was a good contest.'

'Come on you two!' called Dad. 'Get your coats on! The recital starts in just over half an hour.'

Tracy and I sighed in resignation and trudged upstairs to get our coats. I let Tracy go back down the stairs first (in fact I let her reach the bottom first), and then I pretended to trip at the top of the stairs, and tumbled all the way down to the bottom.

Yes, it was dangerous and in ordinary circumstances it would have taken a lot to get me to do something like that. But these were not ordinary circumstances. It wasn't the money (I'd want a lot more than five pounds to fall downstairs); it was my pride and my reputation. I could not allow myself to be beaten by this overdressed Sindy doll. And to have drawn with her would have been to lose. There can be only one winner in a game, and in this game it was going to be me.

I thought I saw a look of awe on her face as I lay in a heap at the bottom of the stairs. I had certainly bruised myself enough to deserve it.

The outcome was that Mum took Tracy to the violin recital, and Dad stayed behind to practise his First Aid on me. I ended up almost disappearing as he enthusiastically stuck plasters all over me and tied me up with bandages. But the main thing was: I had won!

Saturday 9th August

I cannot believe it! I have been conned by that fiend in human shape, that walking fancily dressed lump of bird droppings!

Tracy's parents came and collected her this morning, and as soon as she was gone I went along to the corner shop to pick up the envelope with my winnings from old Mr Carstairs.

I had been expecting some kind of double-cross from Tracy because these last few days have shown me what a cheat and a liar she is. Because of that I had made Mr Carstairs promise not to hand over the envelope to Tracy unless I was with her. This was because I suspected that Tracy might be underhanded enough to forge a note in my name saying he could hand the envelope over to her. (As a safety precaution, I had already forged a note in her name in case it was necessary to get my five pounds back.)

Because I had taken these precautions I thought my money was safe, so you can imagine my shock and horror when I picked up the envelope from Mr Carstairs and opened it. Instead of finding two five pound notes inside it, I found a note from Tracy that read:

Dear Cousin. Well, I won. After all, the bet was to see who was the best dodger, and I have dodged you out of five pounds. I did it by switching the envelope with the money in for this one before we left the house, so I've had the money all the time. By the time you read this I will have spent it.

Better luck next time. Your cousin, Tracy.

I ask you! How low! How despicable! How rotten! What a cheat and a liar and everything rotten and horrible in the world that cousin of mine is!

The worst of it is that I daren't tell anybody the way she cheated me in order to get my money back, because to do so would ruin my reputation as the world's greatest dodger.

I am feeling too sick to write any more. I have been made to look an idiot! I shall have my own back, though. I shall get my parents to take me to visit Tracy and her family, and then watch out!

Other great reads *from* **Red Fox**

Further Red Fox titles that you might enjoy reading are listed on the following pages. They are available in bookshops or they can be ordered directly from us.

If you would like to order books, please send this form and the money due to:

ARROW BOOKS, BOOKSERVICE BY POST, PO BOX 29, DOUGLAS, ISLE OF MAN, BRITISH ISLES. Please enclose a cheque or postal order made out to Arrow Books Ltd for the amount due, plus 22p per book for postage and packing, both for orders within the UK and for overseas orders.

NAME _____

ADDRESS _____

_____

Please print clearly.

Whilst every effort is made to keep prices low, it is sometimes necessary to increase cover prices at short notice. If you are ordering books by post, to save delay it is advisable to phone to confirm the correct price. The number to ring is THE SALES DEPARTMENT 071 (if outside London) 973 9700.

Other great reads from **Red Fox**

THE SNIFF STORIES   Ian Whybrow

Things just keep happening to Ben Moore. It's dead hard avoiding disaster when you've got to keep your street cred with your mates *and* cope with a family of oddballs at the same time. There's his appalling 2½ year old sister, his scatty parents who are into healthy eating and animal rights and, worse than all of these, there's Sniff! If only Ben could just get on with his scientific experiments and his attempt at a world beating *Swampbeast* score . . . but there's no chance of that while chaos is just around the corner.

ISBN 0 09 9750406   £2.50

J.B. SUPERSLEUTH   Joan Davenport

James Bond is a small thirteen-year-old with spots and spectacles. But with a name like that, how can he help being a supersleuth?

It all started when James and 'Polly' (Paul) Perkins spotted a teacher's stolen car. After that, more and more mysteries needed solving. With the case of the Arabian prince, the Murdered Model, the Bonfire Night Murder and the Lost Umbrella, JB's reputation at Moorside Comprehensive soars.

But some of the cases aren't quite what they seem . . .

ISBN 0 09 9717808   £1.99

Other great reads from **Red Fox**

Discover the exciting and hilarious books of Hazel Townson!

THE MOVING STATUE

One windy day in the middle of his paper round, Jason Riddle is blown against the town's war memorial statue.

But the statue moves its foot! Can this be true?

ISBN 0 09 973370 6 £1.99

ONE GREEN BOTTLE

Tim Evans has invented a fantasic new board game called REDUNDO. But after he leaves it at his local toy shop it disappears! Could Mr Snyder, the wily toy shop owner have stolen the game to develop it for himself? Tim and his friend Doggo decide to take drastic action and with the help of a mysterious green bottle, plan a Reign of Terror.

ISBN 0 09 956810 1 £1.50

THE SPECKLED PANIC

When Kip buys Venger's Speckled Truthpaste instead of toothpaste, funny things start happening. But they get out of control when the headmaster eats some by mistake. What terrible truths will he tell the parents on speech day?

ISBN 0 09 935490 X £1.75

THE CHOKING PERIL

In this sequel to *The Speckled Panic*, Herbie, Kip and Arthur Venger the inventor attempt to reform Grumpton's litterbugs.

ISBN 0 09 950530 4 £1.25

Other great reads from **Red Fox**

The latest and funniest joke books are from Red Fox!

THE OZONE FRIENDLY JOKE BOOK
Kim Harris, Chris Langham, Robert Lee,
Richard Turner

What's green and highly dangerous?
How do you start a row between conservationists?
What's green and can't be rubbed out?

Green jokes for green people (non-greens will be pea-green when they see how hard you're laughing), bags and bags of them (biodegradable of course).

All the jokes in this book are printed on environmentally friendly paper and every copy you buy will help GREENPEACE save our planet.

* David Bellamy with a machine gun.
* Pour oil on troubled waters.
* The Indelible hulk.

ISBN 0 09 973190 8   £1.99

THE HAUNTED HOUSE JOKE BOOK
John Hegarty

There are skeletons in the scullery . . .
Beasties in the bath . . .
There are spooks in the sitting room
And jokes to make you laugh . . .

Search your home and see if we are right. Then come back, sit down and shudder to the hauntingly funny and eerily rib-rattling jokes in this book.

ISBN 0 09 9621509   £1.99